CANADIAN SAYINGS

Canadians have more than 135 sayings to indicate stupidity, and here are samples.

Thicker than a B.C. pine.

The wheel is spinning, but the hamster is dead.

He doesn't know if his asshole was punched, bored, or burnt out by lightning.

His intake manifold is sucking air.

Just as happy as if he had brains, isn't he?

Her johnnycake isn't done in the middle.

Not too bright in Toronto: Strong like bull, dumb like streetcar.

He's dead from the arse both ways.

So dumb he thinks Medicine Hat is a cure for head lice.

He's one buttress short of a cathedral.

So inbred, if any kid at the table cries, "Daddy!" all the men stand up.

Sign in his bathroom: "Warning: Objects in mirror are dumber than they appear."

She doesn't know much, but she leads her bowling league in nostril hair.

CANADIAN SAYINGS

1,200 Folk Sayings Used by Canadians

collected & annotated
by

BILL CASSELMAN

McArthur & Company
Toronto

Canadian Cataloguing in Publication Data

    Casselman, Bill
      Canadian sayings: 1,200 Folk Sayings Used by Canadians

    ISBN 1-55278-076-7

    1. Canadianisms (English).* 2. English language — Etymology.
    I. Title.

FC23.C365 1999   422   C98-933096-6
F1006.C365 1999

Composition and Design by Michael P. Callaghan
Typesetting by Moons of Jupiter, Inc. (Toronto)
Cover Design by Tania Craan
Printed in Canada by Transcontinental

McArthur & Company
322 King Street West, Suite 402
Toronto, ON, M5V 1J2

10 9 8 7 6 5 4

for my dear friend, Jack Farr

"Fight, big fighter!"

Contents

INTRODUCTION
Talking the Ears Off a Moose

Here are 1,200 folk sayings used by Canadians. I've collected and annotated them now at the end of the 20th century for two purposes: to give you "a grin as wide as the St. Lawrence" and to preserve them. Many are earthy Canadian originals, like these ten delights:

The puck isn't going his way. *La rondelle ne roule pas pour lui.*

She paddles her own canoe.

Saskatchewan is so flat, you can watch your dog run away from home for a week.

Yukon mosquitoes are so big, they can stand flat-footed and bugger a caribou.

Busier than a Halifax Harbour harlot with the HMCS Toronto in port.

That dude is suckin' slough water. (He doesn't know what he's talking about).

He's lower than whale shit and that's at the bottom of Hudson Bay.

Far as ever a puffin flew.

Gettin' bitched and lookin' for hockey sticks (a trifle tipsy).

It was so cold this morning, before I could take a piss, I had to kick a hole in the air.

WHERE THEY COME FROM
The majority of original Canadian sayings were expressed, naturally, in English and French, with some early borrowing back and forth across linguistic fences. Nowadays, alas, there is less and less knowledge of each other's languages

shared between our two peoples. But both have lively sayings. I think of: "*L'affaire est ketchup,*" 'everything's okay,' or, in a saltier phrase, there is "*pas un pet de travers,*" 'not a fart out of place.' Consider the *pure laine* of this Quebecism: "*Ferme ton gorlot!*" That's a Québécois version of 'shut up' but means literally "stop ringing your sleigh bell."

Later immigrants brought their folklore and ethnic adages to Canada, too. Some of these find their way into Canadian English. For example, from Ukrainian comes this terse Canadian Prairie insult: "Tall like a poplar, stupid like a bean." That is a direct translation from a Ukrainian putdown whose rough transliteration from the Cyrillic to the Roman alphabet is: *visocki yak polya dorni yak fasolya.* "The old woman is sure plucking her geese today" is a wonderful, folksy metaphor to describe a fluffy snowfall, both in English and in the original Ukrainian.

Canadian English has also borrowed folk sayings from Amish and Mennonite German. For example, from the German of farmers near Kitchener, Ontario, comes "*arm wie a Kirchemaus,*" 'poor as a church mouse' (in standard German *arm wie eine Kirchenmaus*) and "*schlau wie die Hille,*" 'slow as the hills.' The last is probably a Mennonite dialect transformation, with attendant alteration of meaning, of the standard German "*schlau wie die Hülle,*" 'sly as the veil.' In Waterloo County in Ontario, one hears "*Schmeile wie ein Klosterkatz,*" 'a smile like a convent cat,' a German-Canadian expression describing contentment. In the old country, nuns and monks fed such cats.

What is a folk saying?

And how do we define it? A folk saying is a humorous, idiomatic phrase or sentence defining some truism of our communal experience, often expressed in non-standard English in the form of a vivid simile or metaphor designed to startle listeners. Folk sayings are passed by word of mouth in a small community where life and work are shared. In this particular collection, a folk saying is not a riddle, a joke, a proverb, a weather rhyme, a folk song lyric, a charm, or a tall tale, although all these are part of a people's oral tradition.

Yes, some sayings begin as salty jokes or statements exaggerated to elicit a laugh. A repeated jest passed down through several generations of a family is well on its way toward enshrinement as a folk saying. Gordon Schmidt of Toronto sent me this example in a grandfather's habitual greeting: "How's your old straw hat?" Generations of children and grandchildren were coached to respond with: "It's never been felt." As the children advance into early puberty, they start to recognize, with a giggle or two, the slightly sexual connotation of the reply, and that helps fix it forever in memory. I do admit that an occasional proverb or rhyme or joke does sneak into my compilation, and stays here because it seems to fit and it's too amusing to leave out.

Why simile and metaphor?

Let's return to part of our definition: "often expressed in non-standard English in the form of a vivid simile or metaphor." Indeed, simile and metaphor are the chief expressive modes of the folk saying. Similes abound: "She's like CPR track. Been laid right across the Prairies." "He fell for her like a blind roofer." Metaphors are everywhere: "He's a hurricane on a ten-cent piece." "There's no grain in that silo." Simile and metaphor are rife in folk sayings, because they are rife in speech. One of the purposes of language, one of the ways we think, is comparison. That's what similes and metaphors do. They permit figurative language like stating likenesses and drawing comparisons. It happens also that the simile is one of the natural mediums to express spoken humour: "He looks like he's been shot at and missed, then shit at and hit." Ordinary speakers understand this, for everyday speech brims with simile and metaphor, and so does the comic writing of the professional humorist.

Satire is another reason we make up and pass on folk sayings. And exaggeration is a common linguistic carrier of satire. Albertans have access to superb beef, and many of them do not like it too well cooked, a fact made plain in this Q&A saying: "Question: How rare would you like your steak? Answer: Just wipe its ass, cut off its horns, and lead it to the table." Comic writers use exaggeration constantly. Consider American comedian Dennis Miller's take on one current neocon nightmare: "Pat Buchanan is so homophobic he blames global warming on the AIDS quilt" (from *The Rants*, Doubleday, 1996).

In folk sayings, the pun is never the lowest form of humour. Based on the similar sound of words and/or their multiple meanings, the pun is important to any spoken saying. A nifty one occurs in this response by a woman to a man boasting of his sexual conquests: "I'm in no mood for an organ recital." A final reason, of course, is this: It's human nature to delight in comic exaggeration of the faults of others. This *Schadenfreude* bristles in many Canadian folk sayings and is the psychological motive force that drives people to create some of them.

WHY ARE SOME SAYINGS IMPROPER?

Folk sayings are not all pleasant and some are earthy enough to offend the prudish. A plain but brave woman venturing into a lumber camp as a cook in southern British Columbia recorded in her diary in 1926 that she overheard this sexist description of her arrival in camp: "Seen the new cook? Ugly? She looks like a dog's ass sewn up with a logging chain." No, they are not pleasant, but they are often what the speaker feels, with all notions of political correctness ruthlessly removed. The violation of some current notion of good taste and the removal of taboo are often what make expressions funny. The semantic shock conveyed in a saying jolts a laugh out of the listener. Every stand-up comic knows that ploy.

Nor is the language of folk sayings suitable for all company. But we are reporting the way real people talked, and still do talk, and so one cannot always gussy up these phrases in Sunday-go-to-meetin' clothes, because such editing-out of unpleasant reference robs folk expressions of their power. Folk sayings may be: off-colour, sacrilegious, mildly disgusting, hugely disgusting. So? The obscene is one mode of everyday talk. And that is my answer to those who are offended or upset that *Canadian Sayings* contains phrases not politically correct. Not politically correct? You betcha! My book is a pie in the face of the constipated propriety that suggests we should not record Canadians' most vivid popular speech.

IMPORTANCE OF ORAL TRADITION

Nowadays such earthiness is largely banned from public media. Print and electronic media are so very fussy about what might offend a small portion of their consumers. The Internet promises to return the right to edit to ordinary people, and so, of course, various professional editors and academics "hoot loudly about too much freedom on the Internet." Although print was a blessed discovery, it has been truly said that print robbed humanity of good memory. Literate societies need to remember less; they can look it up. But word of mouth is still the *fons et origo* of folk sayings. The underground tradition of taboo jokes, naughty limericks, off-colour anecdotes, and risqué ripostes flourishes through oral passing-on. A folk saying that endures and finds its way into print has probably flown from lip to lip for years before it is recorded. Our oral tradition is a powerful safeguard against the repressive censors of the right and the left, the pious busybodies who would purge common speech of its irreverence and pungency. I say: Long may loose lips flap!

How Sayings Begin

Even a few Canadian kilometres alter folk speech. Regan Warner, of Sydney, Ontario, near Huntsville, sent me this observation about different sides of the Ottawa Valley. "On the west side, people might say: 'Lord Liftin' Jesus, that truck's got a lot of snot in 'er!' On the east side: 'Jesus H. Christ, that truck goes like stink!'" And in Ottawa itself: 'Dear me, but that utility vehicle is rather powerful.'

Sometimes we can trace the very beginnings of an expression. But it's only a guess whether or not it will spread from one particular family into the population. Take this expression: "You can't eat pickles in the basement." Dan Roscoe of Winnipeg writes, "My British grandfather, Herbert Parry, was very fond of pickles with his supper. They were normally stored in the basement where it was cool. It often happened therefore that the pickles were overlooked when setting the supper table. Grandfather would say, 'Pass the pickles, please.' Someone would say, 'Oops!' And the forgetful miscreant would be sent down to fetch them. The expression has come down now through two more generations of our family as a generalized saying that means 'what you want is not where you are.' Who knows? If you read it here and use it, this nifty tag may go winging its verbal way across the whole of Canada."

Academic Snootiness

Language scholars have, for the most part, looked upon these lively tags and wise saws as the babble of peasants, and left them out of their studies. In fact, Tom McArthur, a well-known linguist who is the editor of *The Oxford Companion to the English Language* (1992), pins the tail on this particular academic donkey-prejudice when he writes,

"In the use by scholars of such terms as . . . *folk linguistics* there is often a dismissive quality implying that 'folk' movements inherently operate at a lower and therefore less significant level than the traditions to which the scholars themselves belong." Among the delightful exceptions to these pompous snobs who traipse through the wilting groves of academe is T.K. Pratt, professor of English at the University of Prince Edward Island, who, with the help of his students and colleagues, has collected and published *Prince Edward Island Sayings*.

The snobbishness of some wizened eggheads is utter flapdoodle, piffle, and poppycock, for folk sayings give insight into occupations and origins of a community. Folk sayings often preserve in their verbal amber ways of social life, local history, and modes of popular thought. Canadian folk sayings, of course, are not entirely historical. We're still coining doozies. Consider the British Columbia ecologist who says of a dull companion, "He's got his solar panels on the north side." Why, he might be a few sandwiches short of a picnic too. How strong was that Nova Scotia homebrew? "The likker in that jar'd grow hair on a wooden leg in three days."

WHY COLLECT THEM?

But why, you may ask, should we collect these pungent chunks of Canadiana and keep them alive? Well, they are not mere hick talk. In an age where television threatens to make all of us speak exactly the same, in the pale, bland English of the TV newscast, it is no bad thing to keep in circulation these reminders of what a dynamo English can be in the mouths of ordinary Canadians speaking without constraint, without the Thought Police hovering nearby.

Why should you read a folk saying collection? For the laughter? For the sheer ecstasy of knowing? If those answers leave you tepid, nurture this notion: they make great little inserts to pep up a tired speech you may have to deliver. Sales reps find them efficient conversational ice-breakers. They pump vigour into flaccid newspaper copy. Writers of every stripe and persuasion will find ways to make comic points in this treasury of snappers.

Why 1,200 Entries?

In two previous books, *Casselman's Canadian Words* and *Casselmania*, I presented about 400 sayings. Since their publication I have added about 800 expressions to my data-base, and it's time to share them and hope their appearance will solicit more from readers and other collectors.

In this book, there are not multiple entries of the same expression under several different categories. Oh, there are a few. But that somewhat shady compiler's trick was not used extensively here, to bulk up the number of entries claimed. One collection of folk sayings I know does this shamelessly. The offending volume quotes dozens of variations of each saying and then totals them so that its editors can boast of more than a thousand sayings, when in fact there are only several hundred separate and distinct sayings in that book. Although there is scholarly justification for the cataloguing of variations, I have avoided it here in what is a book for popular consumption. My compilation actually contains more than 1,200 *different* folk sayings used by Canadians and is therefore the largest such collection in print at this date.

Categories & CONTRIBUTORS

For their support in bringing this book to press, I thank my agent, Daphne Hart, and my publisher, Kim McArthur. I offer special thanks for cheerful assistance to publicity director Sherie Hodds and the whole team at McArthur & Company. Laser-eyed editor Pamela Erlichman has purged error from five of my books and we are still friends, proof indeed of her patience and love of accuracy. And many thanks to this book's designers, Michael Callaghan and Tania Craan.

For the reader's convenience, I have arranged the folk sayings in broad, numbered categories like Sex, Stupidity, Thinness, and Unpleasantness. The name at the end of an individual entry indicates the person who first submitted the particular saying to me. Their location is stated because it helps denote one area where the expression is used.

Finally, I thank all the Canadians who have helped me haul this harvest into memory's barn, by writing to me, phoning me at radio and TV shows, buttonholing me at book signings, and letting me share their own favourite folksy zingers. If you know a nifty saying not listed here, send it to me at the address given below. I guarantee, I'll have a smile like a butcher's dog.

1. ALL IS WELL

1. A grin as wide as the St. Lawrence.
• Happy indeed, for the river is broad.
  Anne Clarke-Webber, Nelson's Landing, Bedford, Nova Scotia

2. Grinning like a spring salmon in a school of herring.
  Stephen Molloy, Winnipeg, Manitoba

3. Slicker than a brookie!
• Said in answer to "How'd it go?" by an outdoors guide in Alberta. Brookie is a Canadian diminutive for brook trout.

4. *L'affaire est ketchup.*
• Everything's okay, in some Canadian French dialects.

5. *Schmeile wie ein Klosterkatz,* 'a smile like a convent cat' is a German-Canadian expression from Waterloo County in Ontario.
• In the old country, nuns and monks fed such cats.

6. *Pas un pet de travers.* 'Not a fart out of place.'
• That is, everything's in order. The translation is heard among Québec anglophones, and the original is widespread in the various argots of *la belle province*.

7. Smiling like a cracked piss pot.
  Blaine Klippenstein, Sherridon, Manitoba

8. Everything's rosy when the goose hangs high.
• That is, when the harvest is in and the larder is full, this old British expression is apt.

9. Happy as a clam at high tide.
• Common in our Maritime provinces, perhaps
borrowed from early New England colonies.

10. He was grinnin' like a butcher's dog.

11. Happy as a pig in shit.

12. Everything is jake. Everything is jakealoo.
• A number of Canadians remember when this
response to "How are you?" was heard daily. Gordon
Schmidt of Toronto writes, "Jakealoo was in quite
common usage during the 1930s and 1940s in
Hornepayne, the railway divisional point town where
I grew up in northern Ontario. Railway boomers came
from all parts of Canada in those times and brought
their linguistic flavours with them. . . Jakealoo is a
lovely word, understood immediately by all and with
such a musical sound to describe a state of satisfaction
or well-being." E.C. Lougheed, born in 1927 in
Thornbury, Ontario, tells me, "Expressions used by
my father included 'jake,' as in the phrase 'everything
is jake' and my father often added to the word using
the term 'jake-a-loo.'"

The Merriam-Webster's dictionaries state that 1914
is the earliest American citation of "jake" in print. It
then becomes much more frequent in America during
the 1920s and afterward. It was never common in
England, but jake and jakealoo are both heard in
Aussie slang. Jakealoo does not appear in print in
Australia until 1919. Australian and New Zealand
troops probably extended the American jake to mean
okay or fine, and then passed it to Canadian and
American soldiers during the First World War.

In *A Dictionary of the Underworld: British and American,* Eric Partridge points out that jake also appears in print in 1914 in British criminal argot meaning 'familiarity with a secret, state of knowing' and suggests both shades of jake are related ironically to an American colloquialism "a country Jake" which was a synonym for a hick or rural fool. But how does a rube become "fine, okay, in good health?"

Superficially, jakealoo does not appear to be related to jakes meaning "outhouse." But one recalls the dozens of languages in which a response to "How's it going?" is a playful "Shitty, and you?" For example, in German slang the question is asked: *Wie geht's? Alle Scheiße!* 'How's it going? It's all shit!' But the answer is often given with a laugh. Thus it is by no means strange to find a word of excrementitious gist used in everyday speech to signify fine or okay. Perhaps some reader who is privy to the authentic origin of jake will reveal it to us?

13. If I felt any better, I'd throw away my health card.

2. ALL IS NOT WELL

1. The puck isn't going his way.
• From Canadian French: *la rondelle ne roule pas pour lui.*

Alison Hackney, Senneville, Quebec

2. We'll need all hands on deck and the cook.
• This betokened a major emergency at sea in the slang of Grand Banks schooner fishermen. If the cook had to leave the protective cubbyhole of his galley and actually come on deck, then the ship was truly in trouble.

3. There is always something to keep the rabbit's tail short.

Janet Hingley, New Glasgow, New Brunswick

4. Up shit creek without a paddle, or, in a purely Canadian euphemism: up the well-known stream without the necessary means of conveyance.

5. It's better than a kick in the ass with a frozen boot.
• From Fort Francis, Ontario, Dawn Marie Ash offers this advice that things may not be going well, but they could be worse. The saying is also offered to persons who place second or third in contests.

6. Oh, pipes! Or: I got piped!
• This indicates anything negative, like getting hurt or into trouble. It appears to be a regionalism of very restricted locality, but has been reported by several people who grew up in Nobleton and Schomberg, Ontario.

Submitted by Leah Werry, Nobleton.

3. ANGER

1.Wouldn't that frost your tit on a hot day in June?
• Allan Miloff, of Richmond Hill, Ontario, contributed this zesty tribute to annoyance.

2. Cool off in the same skin you got heated up in.
• Originally an Irish saying.

Kathy Noyes, Lloydminster, Alberta

3. She's a temper in search of a tantrum.

Donald Fletcher, Nepean, Ontario

4. I'm so mad, I could spit rust.

5. I couldn't warm up to you if we were cremated together.

6. She went up in the air like a homesick angel.
• I collected this first from Hanna, Alberta, where it was used to describe a person who became angry very quickly. But ex-aviator Don Peters of Smiths Falls, Ontario, writes that it was originally used by pilots to describe the climbing characteristics of fighter aircraft. "She climbs like a homesick angel" was used in comparing planes. If one had flown the CF-100 or the F-86, then one said it of the CF-101 or the CF-104. "Today's pilots," writes Don, "probably say it about the CF-18."

7. I'll be gettin' hot tongue and cold shoulder.
• What a husband arriving home very late is served for supper.

8. Ain't that enough to cramp a snipe!
From New Brunswick.

9. Mad as a bull at a five-barred gate.
Heard in southern Alberta.

10. I'd rather be pissed off than on.

4. APPEARANCE

1. He looks like something that was sent for and didn't come.
• This insult stems from Cape Breton Island, by way of K. Ferguson of Florenceville, New Brunswick, and harks back to the days of the mail-order catalogue.

2. She's a hard-lookin' ticket.

3. His eyes look like two piss-holes in a snowbank.
• Said of someone sleep-deprived or hung-over.

4. She looks like a birch broom in the fits.
• Referring to one frowsy, unkempt, or in the throes of a bad hair day, this saying is heard in every province.

Pamela MacMillan, Charlottetown, Prince Edward Island

5. The porch light is on, but there's nobody home.
• Said of someone who's good-looking but dumb.

6. He had a smile on him like poison come to supper.

7. She's as pretty as a bald-faced heifer.

8. Yellow as a duck's foot.

9. Red as a spanked baby's arse.
• The implication of child abuse has sealed the fate of this folksy simile.

10. Dirty as a duck's puddle.

11. Hard to tell from its looks how far a frog will jump.

12. Straighten up! You look like a pig in a potato garden.

13. You've got a smile like a wave in a slop pail.

14. She was all painted over like a park bench.
• Too much makeup.

Wilhelmine Estabrook, Hartland, New Brunswick

15. Sitting up like a cat shitting in a jug.
• In other words: quite alert!

16. Stop worrying. A man on a galloping horse would never notice.
• Said to persons fussing about their appearance.

G. Lenz, Surrey, British Columbia

17. Looks like she been drug through a knothole backwards.

Linda Boswell, Marshfield, Prince Edward Island

18. Variant: Looks like he was hauled through a knothole and beat with a soot-bag.

Peggy Feltmate, Toronto

19. She's as pretty as a speckled pup in a red wagon.

Tom Kuffel, Grosse Point Park, Michigan

20. He's like a used car with a new paint job: looks okay until you lift the hood.

21. She looks like a hen's arse in pokeberry time.
• Too much lipstick.

22. Cute as a bug's ear.

23. You look like death warmed over.

24. Of a person with a large nose: He could hang from a cherry tree and pick with both hands.

C. Ray, Sault Ste. Marie, Ontario

25. Hunched over like a mouse shitting peach pits.

26. Hunched over like a dog screwing a football.

27. He looks like he's been shot at and missed, then shit at and hit.
• Definitely the worse for wear.

Ken Danchuk, Edmonton, Alberta

28. Variant: He looks like he's been shot at and hit.

Andrea Wall, Grand Falls, Newfoundland

29. All dressed up like a chocolate dog.

5. APPETITE

1. To arrive for dinner "hollow to the neck."
• Guests who came to dinner very hungry in Nova Scotia, ready for a good feed of someone else's cooking, were said to have arrived in such a state.

2. He'll need two assholes to shit that away.
• Of someone who eats a big meal.

3. *J'ai le ventre pardessus de dos* 'My stomach is over my back.'
• A Québec saying contributed by Stephen Vermette that means 'I've eaten too much.'

4. He eats like a starving man but doesn't do enough to break the Sabbath.

Derwyn Evans, London, Ontario

6. BAD LUCK

1. If all hell were raked and the ashes sifted, you could never find a worse bridge hand.
• William Hite of St. Albert, Alberta, contributed his father's line about being dealt a "bust" hand in the familiar card game.

2. He hasn't got a prick's chance in a meat grinder.

Vivian Hansen, Calgary

3. If it was raining soup, he'd be caught with a fork.
• Said of the unlucky in Saskatchewan.

4. "Tough titty" said the kitty, when the milk ran dry.
  Paul Whelan, Unionville, Ontario

5. He's got about as much chance as a one-legged man in an ass-kicking contest.

6. The devil owed her a cake, but paid her a loaf.
• Worse luck than she anticipated came her way.

7. I haven't won a game since Christ left Chicago.
• Loser's slang from bingo games.
  Reported by Diana Campbell of Louisbourg, Nova Scotia.

8. Got no better chance than a one-legged grasshopper in a chicken coop.
  Jean Riddle, Norwich, Ontario

7. BAD MOOD

1. That horse would kick the shortenin' out of a biscuit.
• This was a favourite expression of Alan Young, late cattle boss at the large and famous Pincher Creek Ranch in Alberta, referring to a foul-tempered quarter horse.
  The phrase was submitted by Vance Rockwell of the Canadian Centre for Wolf Research.

2. You've got a face on you like a ripped moccasin.
• Mary de Sousa of Kenora, Ontario, reports her mother's rebuke to a pouting child or to anyone in a hissy fit.

3. They can't scull together.
• Said of two people who can't get along.
Variant: They don't ship together.

Jody Greek, Rose Bay, Nova Scotia

4. Who peed in *your* cornflakes this morning?

5. Can't dance and it's too wet to plough.
• That is, cabin fever may be imminent.

6. He rode in on an ugly horse.
• Said in Alberta of a foul-tempered man.

7. Mean? He wasn't born. He just sprang up one day
after a buzzard jerked off on a hot rock.

Heard in Delta, British Columbia.

8. She could start a fight in an empty house.

9. There's blood for breakfast.
• Brought to Canada by British sailors, this saying was
current by the 1890s in the British navy and originally
referred to a captain's bad mood of a morning.

10. Ornery as an old bear.

11. You've got a face as long as a wet weekend.

12. Ornery as a white heifer.

Glenda Brown, Saskatoon, Saskatchewan

13. Oh, cheer up. It won't always get dark at six.

Mary Anne Sibley, Medicine Hat, Alberta

14. Old bastard! I hope he dies with a hard-on.

15. He has a dog's attitude: if you can't eat it or fuck
it, piss on it.

16. I don't want to live near enough to smell their cabbage cooking.
• Said by a husband about his in-laws.

Jean Riddle, Norwich, Ontario

8. BALDNESS

1. That shiny area isn't baldness. That's the solar panel on a sex machine.

2. You can't grow hair and brains both.

3. You can't grow grass on a busy street.

4. Bald as a bladder of lard.
• Heard infrequently in Nova Scotia, this is a mid-Victorian British expression. A bladder of lard was also used to denote a talkative person.

5. Bald as a peeled onion.

Jean Gibson, Thunder Bay, Ontario

6. Seen more hair on a coconut.

7. Yeah, but in a hundred years, we'll all be bald.

8. Anyone can grow hair, but it takes a real man who suck it back in.

R. Wilkinson, Newmarket, Ontario

9. BLABBERMOUTHS

1. He's got more tongue than a Mountie's boot.

2. She'd talk the ears off a moose.

Rob Russell, St. John's, Newfoundland

3. She's got more lip than a coal bucket.

Wallace Lane of St. John's heard this on the east coast of Newfoundland.

4. That dog can bark a blue breeze.

From Nova Scotia.

5. Her tongue wags like the flapper on a goose's behind.

Donna Tedford, Blue Mountain, Pictou County, Nova Scotia

6. He has his tongue tied in the middle so it can wag at both ends.

Janet Hingley, New Glasgow, New Brunswick

7. He'd talk your head off, then wash your face in the blood.

Jean Riddle, Norwich, Ontario

8. That sermon was longer than forty miles of dirt road.

Wilhelmine Estabrook, Hartland, New Brunswick

9. She could talk all day about one hen.
• This suggests a person with a one-track mind who is also talkative.

10. He runs off at the mouth like a soup sandwich.

Brian Reid, Kemptville, Ontario

11. What a bun struggle!
• Said when a group of older women, their hair worn in buns, are having a highly competitive conversation.

Hedie Epp, Winnipeg, Manitoba

12. You always go around your elbow to get to your thumb.
• Said of incessant, rambling palaver.

Jean Gibson, Thunder Bay, Ontario

13. When he speaks, you never run out of things to listen to.

Joan Gerber, Cambridge, Ontario

14. Shut yer cake-hole.

Margarita Hill, Prince Albert, Saskatchewan

15. From him you'll get more wind than rain.

Frank Gue, Burlington, Ontario

16. She would talk the ear off a tin pail.

17. Ask him the time of day and he'll tell you how to make a watch.

18. She was vaccinated with a gramophone needle.

19. His mouth flaps faster than a loose board on a truck.

20. *Ferme ton gorlot!*
• A Québecois version of "Shut up" but literally "stop ringing your sleigh bell!"

21. Got a mouth on her that moves like a whip-poor-will's ass end.

22. He'd talk the hind leg off a mule, and then whisper in the socket.

23. Empty barrels make the most noise.

24. He'd talk the nuts off a steel bridge.

25. Empty vessels loom biggest.
• This Newfoundland judgment of big mouths is from Bonita Nichols, Summerside, P.E.I.

26. He could talk the ear off a cornstalk.

27. She has a mouth big enough for four rows of teeth.

Arnold Krushel, Morden, Manitoba

28. Joan Hazlett of Cookstown, Ontario, writes: "My grandmother Minnie, of Irish descent from Donegal, when having a satisfying conversation, would always say, 'We're having a good chin-wag' or 'you're a good chin-wagger, my dear.' When she first used the expression to me as a little girl, I didn't get it. She explained, 'Hold your chin with your hand and keep talking.' This is still lots of fun with young children."

10. BODILY FAULTS

1. You're on your beam ends.
• Said to anyone in poor condition, like a ship wrecked at sea that sits on the ends of her beams.

Heard across our Maritimes.

2. He looks like he just ate his Stick Deodorant.
• Said in Northern Ontario of a wimp.

3. Our whole family's got duck's disease: rear ends too close to the ground.
• Said of short stature.

Brenda Brett, Orillia, Ontario

4. Q: Who knit you?
   A: My mother. And she dropped a few stitches.
• This Newfoundland and Irish expression might indicate physical or mental defects.

5. His nose is so big he could stuff it with nickels and have enough money to travel the world.

6. His arsehole stuck out so far, you could have cut pieces off it for washers.
   Ken Danchuk, Edmonton, Alberta

7. He was so bowlegged, he couldn't trap a pig in a ditch.

8. He's so walleyed he can lie on his back and look down a well.
   Wilson Kindred, Brussels, Ontario

9. He looks like he's been ridden hard, and put away wet.

10. He had an ass on him like a tame bee.

11. He won't lie out for lack of a handle to carry him in.
   • Said of a large-nosed person.
   John A.D. McLean, Belleville, Ontario

12. Her ass moves like two rabbits in a bag.

13. Don't stand there, smirkin' like a weasel suckin' eggs through a gumboot.

14. Don't be such a snivelling snuffle-buster.
   Brought to Canada from New Zealand.

15. He had an eye like a stinking eel.
   From Shelburne, Nova Scotia.

16. She's got a face long enough to eat oats out of a churn.

17. She wasn't behind the door when the feet were handed out, was she?

18. Deaf as a haddock.

19. Got sprogs like scows.
• Prince Edward Island expression for someone with big feet or wearing large shoes.

20. You have mailman's eyes: one on the envelope, the other on the mailbox.
• Said of someone walleyed.

21. You have friendly eyes; they always look at each other.

22. She puts her bra on backwards, and it fits.
• Said of a female hunchback.

11. BOONDOCKS

1. Where God buried his socks.

2. Way the hell and gone.

3. It may not be the end of the world, but you can see it from there.
• Susan Jorgenson of Brampton, Ontario, heard this said about Armstrong, a small village at the end of a road north of Thunder Bay.

4. This place is the anus of the earth.

5. This place is the armpit of the known world.

6. They live so far back, they have to keep their own tom-cat.
• From the costly practice of building a farmhouse in the centre of one's land, often necessitating a long road and virtual isolation.

Jean Riddle, Norwich, Ontario

7. You live so far out in the sticks, you gotta wipe the owl shit off the clock to see what time it is.

8. I've been farther around a pisspot looking for the handle than you've been away from home.

12. BRAGGING

1. All her eggs have double yolks.

Reino Kokkila, Etobicoke, Ontario

2. To a braggart: Do you want a medal or a chest to pin it on?

Susan Jorgenson, Brampton, Ontario

3. Prominent? Him? Sure, sticks up like a fresh turd on a frosty morning.

Ken Danchuk, Edmonton, Alberta

13. BURPING

1. It's better to belch it than squelch it.

2. Bring it up again, and we'll vote on it.

3. *Pardon me for being so rude.*
   It was not me; it was my food.
   Instead of staying down below,
   It just popped up to say hello!

• This children's burping rhyme was submitted by Bryan Butcher of Tillsonburg, Ontario.

4. That was well brought up. Too bad you weren't.

5. Your horn seems to work fine. Now try your headlights.

Guy Charbonneau, Timmins, Ontario

14. CANADIANA

These are sayings about provinces, places, and essential Canadian things that were not put into other categories. So it is a kind of Canadian catch-all, but nonetheless delightful because of that.

1. In Canada, we get nine months of winter and three months of darn hard sledding.

2. The CBC cafeteria is the place old flies go to die.

Don Harron, Toronto

Alberta

3. How do mosquitoes breed in Fort McMurray? They slop on a little oil and have sex with Canada geese.

4. To a newcomer: You're talkin' Ontario. You gotta learn to talk Alberta, if you're gonna live out here.

Tom Cameron, Cardston, Alberta

Manitoba

5. So dry last week around Virden, frogs were poundin' on the screendoor, askin' for a dipper of water.

Nova Scotia

6. With Scottish Highlanders, it takes three generations in Canada before they're civilized.

• Said humorously by some Canadians of Highland descent in Nova Scotia.

7. I came from Scotia's Nova where they talk the two talks. Now, I speak Gaelic, and the English twice as more.
• M. McKenzie of Neepawa, Manitoba, remembers a mother born in Pictou County in 1888 boasting thus of her heritage to her children.

Saskatchewan

8. It's so flat in Saskatchewan, you can watch your dog run away from home for a week.

9. It's so flat in Saskatchewan, if you stand on a tall milkcan and look west, you can see the back of your head.

10. It's so flat in Saskatchewan, you can see a train coming for three days.

Dick Swarbrick, Sylvan, Alberta

11. Saskatchewan is the only place in Canada where a woodpecker has to pack a box lunch.

12. Crop's so short this year in Saskatchewan, gophers have to kneel down to eat.

13. You can always tell people from Saskatchewan. When the wind stops blowing, they fall over.

Yukon

14. Yukon mosquitoes are so big, two can carry away a horse.

Shirley Dobie, Dawson Creek, British Columbia

15. Yukon mosquitoes are so big, they can stand flat-footed and bugger a caribou.

15. CERTAINTY

1. That'll show you where the bear stood in the buckwheat.
• In other words, that's proof of what I'm saying.
  Doreen Andreson, Brandon, Manitoba

2. Sure's a gun is iron.
  Mary duManoir, Deep River, Ontario

3. Sure as there's cold shit in a dead dog.

16. CHARITY

1. Charity begins at home, and usually stays there.

2. He'd lend you his arse and shit through his ribs.
• Said of one who is too generous. This expression came over with turn-of-the-century immigrants from Great Britain.

17. CHILDISHNESS

1. That boy never did grow up. One day he just sorta haired over.
• Said when an adult behaves like a child.

18. CHILDREN

1. Go find some snert!
• In southern Saskatchewan, pesky children are sent on a snert-hunt by adults. The child is not told immediately what snert is. Snert = *sn*ow + di*rt*.

2. I'll put a tin ear on you.
• Grandmother to misbehaving children, as she reaches for their ears.

Carole McKenzie, Portage la Prairie, Manitoba

3. If you don't smarten up, I'll slap you down a rabbit hole.
• David Fysh of Thamesville, Ontario, remembers a mother's playful threat to her disobedient children.

4. Those eyes are so big, you could knock them off with a stick.
• In reference to inquisitive children.

5. Mockery said to a pouting child: Nobody loves me. I'm going to the garden to eat worms.

6. You can't howl with the hounds when you still piss like a pup.

Ray Malach, Rose Valley, Saskatchewan

7. Adult to youngster picking his or her nose: Is there going to be a dance?
　　Youngster: No. Why?
　　Adult: Well, you're cleaning out the hall.

8. Mother to demanding child: You no more need that, than a cat needs two tails.

C. Ray, Sault Ste. Marie, Ontario

9. Bored children ask a parent, "What can we do?"
Answer: "Go dicht your neb and flee up."
• That is Scottish advice to go hold your nose and
jump up and down.

Eleanor Hill, Calgary, Alberta

10. Put a cork in your snorkel.
• This began as one family's expression. Shirley Dobie
of Dawson Creek, British Columbia, writes, "When
our son got a snorkel and flippers, I could never get
him out of the man-made lake, until I threatened to put
a cork in his snorkel." It came to mean either (a) don't
engage in an activity to excess or (b) ventures
unacceptable to parents will not be tolerated.

11. I didn't raise my Ford to be a jitney.
• Said when you are disappointed with your children.
A jitney was a ramshackle bus of early 20th-century
America that carried passengers for a cheap fare,
usually five cents.

12. Get out of my way, small change, or I'll spend
you.
• Said to bothersome children, this slangy use of small
change to mean 'children' is common to many
languages. There was a Puerto Rican teenage rock
group once called *Menudo,* which means 'small
change' to *los puertorriqueños.*

13. Every crow thinks his is the blackest.
• Said to parents who boast endlessly about their
children.

14. Keep yer hand over yer ha-penny.
• Ha-penny here means pudendum. This is Scottish

advice to girls going out on their first date. Brought to Ontario by Scottish immigrants.

Morag Condon, London, Ontario

15. Your eyes are too near your bladder.
• Said to a crybaby child.
Variant: Her bladder's too close to her eyes.

16. A silver know-nothing with a whistle on the end.
• When elders are asked by children what they want for Christmas, the adult gives this reply.

17. He's going up Fool's Hill.
• When asked how old an adolescent is, his or her parents may use this reply. Around Shelburne, Nova Scotia, it means he or she is between fifteen and eighteen years old.

18. You're so sweet, you make my teeth ache.
• Said to any child being too smarmy.

Chris Retterath, Moorefield, Ontario

19. CHUTZPAH

Chutzpah is a word in Hebrew, then in Yiddish, for gall, insolence or overweening impudence. The classic example is the man who murders his parents, and then throws himself on the mercy of the court because he is an orphan.

1. She's got more nerve than a canal horse.
• Horses that towed barges along towpaths were notoriously aggressive about not letting other horses or humans near the bank of a canal along which they were towing a barge.

Ray Nobbs of Windsor, Ontario, offers a variant:

More guts than a canal horse.

2. He's got more nerve than a sore tooth.
• One variant is "more nerve than a toothache."

20. CLUMSINESS

1. He couldn't hit water if he fell out of a boat.

Cary Marshall, Thunder Bay, Ontario

2. He left a trail a blind man in a wheelchair could follow in a blizzard.

3. He planted some oak.
• He slipped and fell on the floor. A translation from Manitoba French: *Il a planté du chêne.*

Marcel Lemoine, of Winnipeg, heard this one from a resident of St.-Malo, Manitoba.

21. COMPUTERS

1. He's just a speed bump on the information highway.
• Tim Topham, Dorchester, Ontario, heard this tag for someone who is "Internet-challenged."

22. CONFUSION

1. In and out and all around the rain barrel.

2. Like trying to tell in from out at a Mongolian cluster-fuck.

• Such an event might indeed tax an onlooker's power of analysis.

3. Up and down like a whore's dress.

Ken Danchuk, Edmonton, Alberta

23. CRAFTINESS

1. Slicker than hen poop on a pump handle.

2. Slicker than vaseline on a door knob.

3. Smooth as a stucco bathtub.
• That is, not so crafty as one might think oneself.

4. *Malin comme un pichou.* 'Sly as a lynx.'

5. Slippery as snot on a rooster's lip.

Heard in Whitehorse, Yukon, by Jon Schmidt and contributed by Gordon Schmidt.

24. CRAZINESS

1. Crazy as a bag of hammers.
• The hammers would point in different directions, like a crazy person's train of thought. This may be a development of a British catchphrase recorded as early as 1750 that describes someone who is walleyed: "He has a squint like a bag of nails."

2. Nutty as a fruitcake with the fruit left out.

3. *Avoir des bébites dans la tête.* 'To have bugs in your head,' to be a little crazy.

4. Crazy as a shithouse rat.

5. Crazy as an outhouse mouse.

6. Crazy as Joe Blow's dog jumped in the river to get out of the rain.

J.H. Toop, Windsor, Ontario

7. Two fries short of a Happy Meal™ .
• Deborah Laakso of Thunder Bay, Ontario, suggests this indicates the person is just "a little crazy or weird."

25. CROWDING

1. Living in each other's pockets.
• Said of neighbouring families that are too friendly and too close together.

2. There were thousands and thousands from Tyne Valley alone.
• This localism, belonging solely to Prince Edward Island, is comic exaggeration to describe a very small crowd.

3. A variant of 2 from Nova Scotia's South Shore: There was t'ousands and t'ousands of them, maybe even hundreds.

26. DEATH

1. Gone to the Sand Hills.
• A southern Alberta euphemism for death. The Sand Hills are the Happy Hunting Grounds for the Blood people of the sandy hill country south of Lethbridge.

2. Taking a dirt nap in the bone orchard.
• Dead and buried.

3. *Pèter au fret.* 'To fart in the cold' = to die, in lively Québecois folk speech.

4. His bungee cord is frayed.
• One more "jump" will kill him. He is near death.
   Helen King, Vermilion, Alberta

5. My, she got away in a hurry.
• A description of sudden death, heard at a funeral in Chesterville, Ontario.

6. Sympathy cards? Lord, yes, we got enough to shingle hell over twice.
   Peggy Feltmate quotes her great-great-aunt Zenia of Guysborough County, Nova Scotia.

7. He's sucking on daisy roots.

8. She's in her pine overcoat.

9. It isn't the cough that carries you off,
   It's the coffin they carry you off in.
   Mary and Rick Humphrey, Wasaga Beach, Ontario

10. Heavier than a dead minister.
• When a local reverend passed on, everyone in the parish wanted to be a pallbearer.

27. DEFECATION & URINATION

1. He went for a dump and the gophers got him.
• Said of anyone lost on the prairies.

2. Common as cat shit and twice as nasty.

3. He's as fine a fellow as ever shit over the heel of a boot.
• Heard in the Ottawa Valley.

4. Got the backdoor trots.
• Diarrhea in the days of the outhouse.

5. I had the shits so bad, I could split a shingle at fifty paces.

6. I could shit through the eye of a needle.
• Said by one afflicted with diarrhea.

7. I have to go and wring my mitt.
• Man excusing himself to go to outhouse for a pee.
  From Guysborough County in Nova Scotia.

8. I'm going to water the lilies.

9. I'm off to tap a kidney.

10. I've got to shake hands with the bishop.

28. DIFFICULTY

1. Harder than getting out of hell without claws.
  Colleen Farrell, Head of Chezzetcook, Nova Scotia

2. Just remember, you can't get manure from a rocking horse.

29. DISMISSAL & USELESSNESS

1. I shot better men than you for a dollar-fifty a day.
• World War II veteran's judgment of certain persons

he met upon returning to Canada after the war.

Linda Olson, Gimli, Manitoba

2. Make like a hockey player and get the puck outa here.

Charlene Dobie, Surrey, British Columbia

3. Go peddle your fish.
• Christian Carpenter, Corunna, Ontario, remembers childhood in rural New Brunswick where "kids quite often took some of the catch and strung them on the handlebars of their bicycles, then rode around the neighbourhood and sold them to neighbours who were not commercial fishermen." The saying was a common dismissal by adults of pestering children.

4. May a duck kick you!
• This Ukrainian dismissal (basically it means 'buzz off') sounds better even in a rough transliteration from Ukrainian: *nekxai tebe kochka kopne!*

From Theresa Zolner.

5. *Va pèter dans le trèfle.*
• Go fart in the clover; *c'est-à-dire*, piss off.

6. *Va donc pétaler dans les fleurs.*
• Go pick the petals off flowers, that is, buzz off.

Guy Charbonneau, Timmins, Ontario

7. Go to Halifax!
• Canadian and British naval curse. A minced oath for "go to hell!" But British use recalls the Elizabethan beggars' prayer: "From Hull, hell, and Halifax, Good Lord deliver us" (in print by A.D. 1586).

"Go to Halifax" could mean "go and be hanged." This refers to an actual bit of historical legislation in

the Yorkshire cloth-making town of Halifax. On this
side of the Atlantic briny, our Nova Scotian capital
was named in 1749 after George Montagu Dunk, Earl
of Halifax, a prominent merchant of 18th-century
Nova Scotia. Back in Merry Olde England, the Halifax
Gibbet Law provided severe penalty for anyone caught
stealing goods worth more than 13 1/2 pennies, namely
beheading on the Halifax gibbet. Now this gibbet, a
renowned and lethal piece of municipal ordnance, was
unique in England in that it resembled closely a
French guillotine. The law, repealed in 1650,
originated as a local attempt to thwart theft of cloth
left drying on open racks at Halifax.

Naturally then, Elizabethan vagabonds targetted
Halifax when in need of "a nice bi' o' stuff." The
severe law gave rise to the myth that at Halifax the
captured miscreant was hanged first, and then after the
necktie party, a brief inquiry was held to determine
what precisely he had done wrong. "From Hull, hell,
and Halifax, Good Lord deliver us" indeed. Thieves
and wanderers shunned the British town of Hull
because citizens there made beggars do manual labour
in order to earn food. The rope of choice for the
gallows was braided of sturdy strands of neck-cracking
hemp, hence the origin of a grisly old English phrase:
to die of a hempen fever = to be hanged.

8. Shove it up the highest rafter of your ass!

9. I'd know your hide in a tannery.

10. He just went around the corner with a rat in his
mouth.

• When asked where someone worth dismissing is.

11. She'd give a dog's arse heartburn.

12. Useless as casters on a crutch.

13. Useless as tits on a boar hog (or a bull).

14. Useless as a whip-socket on a car.
• The whip-socket was a metal or wooden cylinder attached to the dashboard of any horse-drawn vehicle into which the handle of the whip was inserted when the whip was not being used.

15. Useless as a spare prick at a wedding.

16. Useless as a fart in a thunderstorm.

17. As small as a dimple on a pimple on a sand flea's arse.

18. That's hail on a tin roof.
• Said to dismiss what someone has said as meaningless noise.
  E.C. and G.I. Lougheed

19. He's lower than a snake's belly in a wagon rut.
• From Three Hills, Alberta.

20. Go to hell and pump thunder!
• A dismissal that suggests the hearer does not believe the speaker.

21. He's not fit to carry guts to a bear.

22. That dog won't hunt.
• The same old tired trick, physical or verbal, will not work. An American folk expression from the southern states, but heard in Canada too. It was used by President Bill Clinton in his first presidential debate with Republican presidential candidate Bob Dole on

Sunday Oct. 6, 1996. Dole used the "golden oldie" Republican chop of calling Clinton a liberal. The President smiled broadly and said, "I just don't think that dog will hunt this time."

23. Did your mother have any children that lived?

24. Go put an egg in your shoe and beat it.

From Wendy Mewhort, quoting her stepfather.

25. That's a small thing in a big outfit.

A saying of Tom Farnsworth of Valhalla Centre, Alberta, submitted by his son-in-law, Dave McRae of Grande Prairie, Alberta.

26. He's too heavy for light work, and too light for heavy work.
• A farmer sizes up a young hand.

27. You're lower than a gnat's armpit.
• Wilhelmine Estabrook of Hartland, New Bruswick, points out that this saying could be used in the first person as well, to express shame.

28. You're so low, you could walk under a door with a Stetson on and never bend a knee.
• A Stetson is a large cowboy hat.

Shirley Schwartz, Regina, Saskatchewan

29. He should be dragged out into the street and shot with a ball of his own shit.

Ken Danchuk, Edmonton, Alberta

30. Go shimmy up a gum tree.

Jean Day, Sarnia, Ontario

31. You ain't worth the round of ammo it would take to shoot you.

32. *Baise-moué l'ail!* 'Kiss my ass!'
• Literally 'kiss my garlic.'

33. Go piss up a rope and play with the steam.

34. Go shit in your hat, pull it over your ears, and call it curls.

35. You don't know frog shit from pea soup.

36. Your wife has marital thrombosis. She married a clot.
• A low pun on "clod."

37. Useless as pyjamas on a bride.

30. DISTANCE

1. Just a hen's race from here.
• A short distance, because chickens can only run a short distance at high speed.

2. Far as ever a puffin flew.
  From Newfoundland.

3. You can't tell how far a grasshopper can jump just by looking at him.
• First impressions are not always correct, whether you are judging people or distance.
  Angus McAuley, Surrey, British Columbia

31. DISTRUST

1. He's so sneaky, I wouldn't trust him in a shithouse with a knife and fork.

2. Fine words butter no parsnips.
• This is distrust of high-flown promises that turn out
to have meant nothing. The saying is British and
recorded as early as 1750.

3. He'd steal anything but a red-hot cookstove or an
alder swamp.
• From New Brunswick's Miramichi area.

Roberta Richardson, Riverview, New Brunswick

32. DRESS

1. They're out today in their figures.
• That is, folks have taken off their bulky winter
clothes and now in fair weather one can see what their
bodies look like.

2. All dressed up like a spare bedroom.

3. It's snowing down south.
• Said when a lady's slip is showing.

4. All dolled up like a barber's cat.
• This is a late 19th-century Canadianism. Never saw
such a fancy feline, myself.

5. Neat but not gaudy, as the devil said when he painted
his arse pink, and tied up his tail with pea-green
ribbon.
• 19th-century British.

6. He stands out like a clown at the wake.

Donald Fletcher, Nepean, Ontario

7. All dressed up like a chocolate dog.

Heard in Peterborough, Ontario.

8. I wouldn't wear that to a dog fight.

Jean Gibson, Thunder Bay, Ontario

9. There wasn't enough clothes on her to flag a hand-car.
• Said of a scantily clad female.

A phrase of the late Boyd Beacock, a CPR conductor from Chapleau, Ontario, reported by his brother-in-law George Fairfield of Toronto.

10. She fell into a rag bag and got out dressed.

11. It's four o'clock in the button factory.
• In the prezipper days when men's trousers had buttons, this remark indicated that some of the buttons on the fly of trousers were undone. Another notice of this condition was to tell a gentleman that he was "flying low."

Beatrice Stevenson, Wellesley, Ontario

12. Flashy! Like a rat with a gold tooth.

33. DRINKING ALCOHOL

1. Gettin' bitched and looking for hockey sticks.
• That is, getting drunk.

Brent Haig of Sudbury heard this one in Lindsay, Ontario.

2. The only thing you mix with good rum is spit.

Ron Keough of Sydney, Nova Scotia, offers this Cape Breton Island saying.

3. Water your lawn with beer and gin, and it will come up half cut.

Gladys Carter, Halifax, Nova Scotia

4. Eyes like piss-holes in snow.
• Said of a hung-over person.

5. Eyes like two cherries in a bucket of shit.

6. Close your eyes or you'll bleed to death.
• To a hung-over person.

7. To be sicker, I'd have to be bigger.
• Said by someone hung-over.
  Charlie Corkum, Summerside, P.E.I.

8. Got the Gobis.
• When your mouth is as dry as the Gobi desert after a long night of drinking.
  From Grand Falls, Newfoundland.

9. The zacklies.
• When your mouth tastes exactly like your arsehole.

10. A jug of real porch-climber.
• That is, a bottle of cheap wine.
  Heard in Kirkland Lake. Guy Charbonneau, Timmins, Ontario

11. He was all fucky-toed, like a blind horse in a pumpkin patch.
• No doubt, that would be your stumbling inebriate.

12. He's got his snowsuit on and he's heading north.
  From northern Manitoba.

13. That hootch would raise a blood blister on a leather boot.
  Heard in Whitehorse, Yukon.

14. Strong enough to grow hair on a wooden leg in three days.
• Said of potent home brew in Campbell's Bay, Québec.

15. He's got Brewer's Droop.
• Said in Ontario of a man who has drunk too much and cannot perform sexually.

16. *Avoir mal aux cheveux.*
• To be so hung-over that you are having a 'hair ache.'

17. Your eyes look like two cherries in a bowl of buttermilk.

18. Wine's in, wit's out.

19. I'm so dry, I'm fartin' dust.

20. I feel like a cat had kittens in my mouth.
• This describes the disagreeable symptom of a hangover when one's tongue feels "furry."

21. She has a brick in her hat.
• She's a little top-heavy with hootch and staggering. British, from 1870 onward.

22. He was on his third drink and feelin' like a man should the year round.

   Wilhelmine Estabrook, Hartland, New Brunswick

23. Eyes like peach pits.

24. Your eyes look like road maps.
• All those little, filamentary red lines criss-crossing the white of the conjunctiva suggest that you have quaffed too much of the amber distillate.

34. EARLINESS

1. To be up a crow piss.
• To be up early in Prince Edward Island.

2. To arise at first sparrow fart.

Heard in King City, Ontario.

35. EASE

1. Easy as picking fly shit out of pepper with boxing gloves.

2. Easy as nailing Jello™ "to plastic wallpaper."

3. Easy as driving a herd of bees through a snowstorm with a cow switch.

4. Easy as opening an oyster with a bus ticket.

36. EMBARRASSMENT

1. I'm sweatin' like a whore in confession.

2. Redder than a turkey's ass at cranberry time.

3. Blush like a black dog.

37. EQUANIMITY

1. It's better than a poke in the eye with a sharp stick.

Ron Bronson, Waterloo, Ontario

2. It's better than a kick in the head with a frozen boot.

3. It's better than a slap on the belly with a dead fish.

4. Don't go getting your knickers in a twist.

5. It's not as green as it's cabbagey-looking.

Jacqueline (Gaudette) Dysart, Espanola, Ontario

6. *Mange-toi du pain blanc.* 'Eat your white bread.'
• Sometimes said in Québec French when a situation is only going to get worse. Enjoy what you have before you.

7. It's better than a kick in the ass with a frozen mukluk.
• Used by Canadian soldiers on northern postings.

Ken Hansen, Saskatoon, Saskatchewan

8. You know what they did in the old days when it rained? They let it rain.
• There is no point in worrying about what you cannot control.

A saying of Tom Farnsworth of Valhalla Centre, Alberta, submitted by his son-in-law, Dave McRae of Grande Prairie, Alberta.

9. Better than a poke in the eye with a frozen mackerel.

Jean McLeod, Victoria, British Columbia

10. Leave her lay where Jesus flang her.
• A Newfoundlandism now heard throughout the Maritimes.

Daniel Noonan, Sidney, British Columbia

11. *Ça ne me pèse pas une fraise dans le cul d'un ours.* 'That isn't worth a strawberry in a bear's ass to me.'
• That is, I couldn't care less.

From Les Éboulements on the north shore of the St. Lawrence River. Alison Hackney, Senneville, Québec

38. EUPHEMISM

1. "Rather than call someone a bastard, my father
would say, 'His aunt had him to a boarder.'"

So writes Alex Dixon of Duncan, B.C.

39. EVIL

1. He has a heart as black as the Earl of Hell's riding
boots.
• Irish settlers first brought this saying to Nova Scotia
in the 18th century. But it is recorded in England in
the 17th century. Sometimes it's the Earl of Hell's
vest. And it refers to any object, deed, or feeling of
Satanic hue that grabs the speaker's attention.

Gale Woodall, Elmira, Ontario

40. EXCUSES

1. Excuse me for livin'. I musta fell out of a hearse.
• This was the favourite expression of an Ursuline nun
who taught at Tecumseh, Ontario, and it was sent in
by several of her former students.

2. Jabbering like a devil in holy water.
• A translation from Canadian French *'comme un
diable dans l'eau bénite.'* Henriette Bossé of New
Brunswick points out that this is a perfect description
of modern-day political spinmeisters, blabbing away
to the media for the purpose of damage control after
some politician has put his foot in his mouth or put a

somewhat more private portion of his anatomy in a place it might have been wiser to shun.

41. FAILURE

1. There was a hill to climb, and he didn't have the right boots.
• A translation from Swedish.
Heard in Saskatchewan.

42. FAKERY

1. Phony as a three-dollar bill.

2. Fake as Canadian diamonds or *aussi faux que les diamants Canadiens.*
• When Jacques Cartier returned to France in 1542 after a third voyage to the new world, he sailed home with barrels of rocks that he thought contained diamonds and gold. He was merely the first European to be fooled by those twinkling tricksters of geology: quartz and iron pyrite (fool's gold). Continental French still has the expression.

43. FAREWELLS

1. See you, Lord willing, and the creek don't rise.
A prairie bye-bye submitted by Linda Darwent.

2. Come back again when you can't stay so long.
Germaine Hornsby, Lunenburg, Nova Scotia

3. It's been a slice!
• It was a good time. Correspondent Wayne Morgan explains that "a slice" was any piece of sweet pastry brought to a church bake sale, described by its shape, not by its content.

4. If I don't see you tomorrow, I'll see you through the window.
• Brent Haig of Sudbury heard this farewell in Lindsay, Ontario, suggesting that if I don't see you soon, I'll see you in passing.

5. We're off in a cloud of flying hen shit.

44. FATNESS

1. He's got a gut like a harbour tomcod.
• A fat fish indeed.
Mike Reid, Corner Brook, Newfoundland

Geez, I'm just like the harbour tomcod, all blown up.
John Ducey supplied this Newfoundland variant.

2. He's as big around as a puncheon.
From Newfoundland.

3. Two axe handles and a plug of chewing tobacco across the behind.
• Wide hips bring this unkind assessment.
Carol Aubé, Barrie, Ontario

4. He's got more chins than a Chinese phonebook.
Dick Swarbrick, Sylvan, Alberta

5. He looks like two section men in a clinch.

• Prairie railway lingo.

Martin Prentice, Drayton Valley, Alberta, reports this saying of his father born in Pense, Saskatchewan.

6. To flub the chub.
• To pinch someone where they are fat.
• Young male teenagers' expression, popular in Ontario during the 1970s and 1980s.

Susan Jorgenson, Brampton, Ontario

7. She's beef to the ankles.

Jean Riddle, Norwich, Ontario

8. He's got a gut on him like a poisoned pup.

Contributed by Marjorie Andrews quoting Old Jack, her late neighbour in the Coboconk-Burnt River area of Ontario.

9. He's as fat as mud.
• That is, healthy. The simile is cited as early as 1864 by John Geikie in his *George Stanley; or, Life in the Woods*, in a part of the pioneer memoir where the speech of early Canadian settlers is discussed.

45. FEAR

1. *Ich wunsch' ich wäre daheim, und der Hund wär da.* 'I wish I were at home and the dog were here.'
• Joan Gerber of Cambridge, Ontario, submitted this German expression from the Amish and Mennonite community of Waterloo County. It means: I fear what I have to do and what is plainly before me and is my duty to do.

46. FLATULENCE

1. I'm so dry, I'm farting dust.

Jean Wendren, Tisdale, Saskatchewan

2. Whenever you be, let your wind blow free.

Marilyn Brewer, Mill Cove, Hubbards, Nova Scotia

3. Better out than in a poor man's eye.
• Said after breaking wind:

Ron Brown, Durham, Ontario

4. He's shooting bunnies.
• Nursery term for farting.

5. Your cough sounds better.

6. Your voice is deeper, but your breath smells the same.
• When someone farts twice.

7. Funny as a fart in a space suit.

8. The fox smells his own hole.
• Said to the accuser when one is accused of just breaking wind.

9. Not bad for a half-inch woofer.
• Said when an audiophile breaks wind.

10. Speak, O toothless one!
• Said when someone breaks wind.

11. An empty house is better than a bad tenant.

12. Disappeared faster than a fart in a dancehall.

13. He could outfart the Old Fart himself.

14. *Pas un pet de travers.* 'Not a fart out of "place."'
• That is, everything's in order.

15. *Se pèter les bretelles.* 'To fart off your suspenders.'
• To burst with pride.

16. The fartin' horse will never tire.
    The fartin' man's the one to hire.

17. He was all over the place like a fart in a glove.

18. Small boy: My bum is asleep.
    Grandfather: Yep. I hear it snoring.

19. Better to fart and bear the shame than not to
fart and bear the pain.
• The folk myth claims that this was the
instantaneous retort of a courtier accused of breaking
wind in the presence of Queen Victoria who was,
naturally and by regal prerogative, not entirely
amused.

20. "Book!' he says, and can't read a paper yet.
• Said after a child has broken wind and based on the
British perception that the sound of the word *book* has
a flatulent air about it.

47. FOOD & COOKING

1. When the tide's out, the table's set.
   A Haida saying, contributed by Kate Weathrill, Ottawa.

2. Q: How rare would you like your steak?
   A: Just wipe its arse; cut off its horns; and lead it to
the table.

• An Alberta recipe for rare meat from S. Rabbitte of Calgary.

3. To get a better piece of chicken, you'd have to be a rooster.

4. I've seen a cow hurt worse than that get better.
• On being served beef that is too rare.

Garth Goddard of Toronto quotes his father, Stan.

5. What's for supper? Rabbit tracks and wind pudding.
• Susan Milankov thinks this response of her mother may be a translation from New Brunswick Acadian French.

6. Tastes bad enough to turn a cow from her oats.

7. That grub goes around your heart like a hairy worm.
• Hearty foods that stick to your ribs earn this praise in some Scottish dialects.

Ian Mennie, Fredericton, New Brunswick

8. If there's a lot, eat a little. If there's a little, eat it all.

Andria Wushke, Rocanville, Saskatchewan

9. Meat's so tough, you couldn't poke a fork in the gravy.

Irene Lucioia, Redwater, Alberta

10. Offered too much food: No thanks, I'm up to pussy's bow.
• This is Australian, in reference to the bow around a kitten's neck.

11. No thanks, I'm up to dolly's wax.
• Australian. Dolls once had wax faces.

Nansi Cox, London, Ontario

12. What's for supper? "Shit with sugar."
• Pestered cooks once used this reply.

13. She couldn't parboil shit for a tramp.

Joe Wall, Grand Falls, Newfoundland

14. Was the fruit fresh? Well, it was upperclass. The strawberries had fur coats.

Jean Gibson, Thunder Bay, Ontario

15. You may be chasing a crow for that before spring.
• Mother to a child who is a finicky eater and refuses a particular food.

Anne Clarke-Webber, Nelson's Landing, Nova Scotia

16. Full as an egg.

17. Butter is contrary twice a year.
• You can churn and churn, and sometimes, things just won't "set" right.

Jean Riddle, Norwich, Ontario

18. He's a dab hand at a camp stove; makes bannock so thin it's only got one side to it.

19. I've passed roadkill better done than this.

20. May his whiskers grow green when he eats a crubeen.
• Crubeen is Irish, like this pleasant wish with its implication that tasting food from one's homeland will make one fondly nostalgic. The word is one gift from Irish immigrants to Newfoundland. *Crúibín* is the

diminutive of *crúb* 'hoof' and means a pig's trotter, usually pickled in salt and boiled. Crubeen is the hock of a pig's foot, the joint between the tibia and the little bones of the foot.

H.M. Balint, Fonthill, Ontario

21. This food is so bad it would harelip a dog.

22. Her cookin' is so bad the flies are taking up a collection to mend the hole in the screen door.

23. She's awful clever with a bite.
• Said of a good cook in Chipman, New Brunswick.
From Lauchlan Fulton.

24. I'm so full, I feel like I'm going to have a batch of dead ones.

25. What's for dessert? Wait-and-see pudding!
• Said by the cook to inquiring children.

26. What's for supper? Bread and pull-it.
• A pun on pullet or chicken?

27. Two tall Swedes couldn't shake hands over that plate.
• Said of a big helping of food on farms around Irma, Alberta.

28. Gone over a goodish piece of grass.
• Said of tough mutton, implying it's meat from a very elderly sheep.

29. I am sufficiently sophonsified that another bite would be obnoxious.
• *Sophonsified* has a resonant and authoritative ring to it. It is, unfortunately, utterly spurious as a learned word. I have never found it in a dictionary. It must be

a nonce word, conceived by some anonymous and deft word-coiner, and passed down by word of mouth.

30. Can you get outside of all that?
• Said to someone sitting down to a very large serving of food in our Maritimes. Can you eat the whole plateful?

Ron Grant, Saint John, New Brunswick

31. There's only two things you get out of life, and one of them's eating.

Tom Farnsworth and Dave McRae, Grande Prairie, Alberta.

32. A fish with no bones is like a land with no stones.

48. FORGETFULNESS

1. My head will never save my heels.

Marguerite Hill, Barrie, Ontario

49. FRECKLES

1. Freckles? Looks like she swallowed a dollar and broke out in pennies.

2. You must have gotten your tan through a screen door.

3. He was christened by a baker.
• Big freckles resemble bran splotched on the face of one baking.

4. A horse must have farted bran in his face.

Charlie Corkum, Summerside, P.E.I.

50. FRUSTRATION

1. Oh, balls on a bowlegged goose!
• Dixsie Wildin, of Lloydminster, Alberta, recalls her mother's exclamation of exasperation.

2. I could chew a nail in two.

3. He gives me a pain where a pill can't reach it.
   Kate O'Donnell, Brantford, Ontario

51. FUN

1. We're gonna raise hell and block it up with a chip.

2. I ain't had so much fun since my young brother got et by the hogs.
• This one is in print by 1850 in the United States.
   Donald Hossack, Trenton, Ontario

3. Fun's fun, but pork is a pig's ass.
• That is, let's get serious and deal with the issue at hand.
   Susan Jorgenson, Brampton, Ontario

52. GINGERLINESS

1. Grinnin' like a mule eatin' cockleburrs.
   Ken Danchuk of Edmonton, Alberta, offers a variant:
Smiling like a mule eating thistle.

2. Smiling like a fox chewing bumblebees.

3. Grinning like a skunk eating bumblebees.
   Wilhelmine Estabrook, Hartland, New Brunswick

4. You've got a grin like a Cheshire cat eating shit off a hot stove.

• The Cheshire cat is a character in Lewis Carroll's *Alice in Wonderland*. Its contented smile indicated some secret amusement. Folklore's coprophagic addition to Carroll's simile alters the meaning to suggest a false smile or a smile that hides an unpleasant reality.

53. GOOD LUCK

1. Luckier than a dog with two arseholes.

Douglas Warren, Blumenort, Saskatchewan

54. GOSSIP

1. His tongue is so long, he can lick his own asshole.

2. That woman's got more news than a dog's got fleas.

Wilhelmine Estabrook, Hartland, New Brunswick

55. GREETINGS

1. Q: How's your old straw hat?
   A: It's never been felt.

56. HASTE & SLOWNESS

1. Faster than you can say, "Jack Miner's geese."

• Karen Watson heard this one in southwestern Ontario near Jack Miner's bird sanctuary at Kingsville, Ontario.

2. Slow as cold molasses running uphill.
Variant: Slower than molasses in January running uphill.

3. He moved as fast as a fart through a keg of nails.
Barney Moorhouse, Bancroft, Ontario

4. Slower than the second coming of Christ.

5. Steppin' faster than a hen on a hot griddle.
Janet Hingley, New Glasgow, New Brunswick

6. They're off like the bride's undies.

7. Faster than the milltails of Hell.
• From Nova Scotia and many other locales in Canada. E.C. Lougheed, who was born in the Georgian Bay town of Thornbury, writes that there was a dam with a mill there and later a hydro-electric power plant and much use of the "milltails of Hades" expression.

8. Going like Torchy Peden.
• That is, riding very fast on a bicycle. Peden was a champion Canadian cyclist.

9. *Schlau wie die Hille.* 'Slow as the hills.'
• A German-Canadian expression from Waterloo County, Ontario, this is probably a Mennonite dialect transformation, with attendant alteration of meaning, of the standard German *schlau wie die Hülle,* 'sly as the veil.'

10. He could step dance faster than a cat could lick its ass.

11. The hurrier I go, the behinder I get.
Heard in Meaford by Kirk Miller.

12. He talked so slow you could walk between the words.

Kerry Hill, Marystown, Newfoundland

13. Hold her, Knut, she's headin' for the barn.

14. If the dog hadn't stopped for a shit, he might have caught the rabbit.

15. Jumpin' around quicker than a flea on a hot griddle.

16. Shivering like a dog shitting herring bones.

Joe Wall, Grand Falls, Newfoundland

17. She was up those stairs like a rat up a sewer pipe.

George Fairfield, Toronto

18. Pounced on that like a duck on a June bug.

57. HATRED

1. I hope you get lockjaw and have to vomit.

2. I hate you so much that, when you pass my gate, I wish you'd run.

Gay Kurtz, Woodrow, Saskatchewan

3. Your mother should have held her waters and drowned you while she had the chance.

Jennifer Hancharuk, Sioux Lookout, Ontario

58. HELPING

1. I wouldn't piss in his ear if his brains were on fire.
• Contributed by genial former *Toronto Star* word

columnist Lew Gloin, who states that it was heard circa 1961 in the composing room of the *Hamilton Spectator* when a supervisor asked a favour of an inferior.

Ken Danchuk of Edmonton, Alberta, offers this variant:

I wouldn't piss up his ass if his guts were on fire.

2. Don't tell me how to drive my own hayrack around my own farm.

From Ukrainian. Thanks to Theresa Zolner.

3. Every little bit helps, as the man said when he pissed in the millpond.

Janet Hingley, New Glasgow, New Brunswick

59. HONESTY & DISHONESTY

1. He's as crooked as a nine-turn road.

Graham Butler, Clarenville, Newfoundland

2. So crooked, he could hide behind a spiral staircase.

Garth Goddard of Toronto heard this in Halifax.

3. Duck soup! If I had another spoon, I'd eat more of it.
• On hearing fibs or tall tales.

Sherri Rothwell, La Salle, Manitoba

4. He's suckin' slough water.
• He knows nothing of what he's talking about.
Slough water was unclean and unfit to drink, as opposed to well water which was potable.

Dennis Purschke, St. Albert, Alberta

5. He's so crooked, when he dies they'll have to screw him into the ground.

6. So crooked, he can't lie in bed straight.

From Ken Danchuk, Edmonton, Alberta

7. As crooked as a dog's hind leg.

8. So dishonest, if he thought Christ had been taken from the Cross, he'd steal the nails.

Jean Riddle, Norwich, Ontario

9. Always one skedaddle ahead of the bailiff.

10. He's so crooked, he has to sleep on a warped board.

11. He's so low, he'd have to climb a ladder to kiss a snake's belly.

12. Straight as a loon's leg.
• That is, honest, in Nova Scotia.

13. Twisted as a ram's horn.
• Not quite so honest in Nova Scotia.

14. Honest as the day is long.

15. When the sun shines on the righteous, the rest of us get some too.

Tom Farnsworth, Valhalla Centre, Alberta

16. He's so low, he can suck a centipede's dick without bending his knees.

17. He's lower than whale shit, and that's at the bottom of Hudson Bay.

From Churchill, Manitoba.

18. You could look up a snake's asshole and think it's the North Star.
• Now that would place one in quite an abject condition.

19. Trust him, but never pick up the soap if you're in the shower with him.

60. HOSPITALITY

1. I'm at home myself and wish you were all there.
• Said playfully by a host at table. Presumably, if you all were there, that is, at your own homes, the host would be less burdened by the need to be hospitable.

Jack Rogers, Windsor, Ontario

2. Sit down for an hour; it won't take you a minute.

Margaret Todd of Winnipeg remembers this saying of her father-in-law who hailed from Prince Edward Island.

3. After three days, both fish and guests start to stink.

Arlene Robinson, Winnipeg, Manitoba

4. You invitin' them? Careful. They stay on and on until the last dog is hung.

Kevin McIntyre, Saskatchewan

61. HUNGER

1. There were more mealtimes than meals in those days.
• Audrey Godbout of Cap Rouge, Québec, recalls this rueful saying from the Gaspésie.

2. I'm so hungry I could eat the hind leg off the lamb of God.

Joe Wall, Grand Falls, Newfoundland

3. I'm so hungry my stomach thinks my throat is cut.

4. I could eat a skunk through a screen door with chopsticks.

Mary Jane Goddard, Parlee Brook, New Brunswick

5. Hungry? I could grab the slack of my belly and wipe my eyes with it.
• This is a nautical catchphrase from the British merchant marine of the late 19th century.

6. I'm so hungry I could eat a dead skunk through a screen door with a toothpick.

Attributed to John E. Potter, a farmer near Woodstock, Ontario, submitted by his son John, of Ridgeville, Ontario.

7. It's been a pig's picnic.

Father Keith Whittingham, St. Barnabas Church, St. Catharines, Ontario

8. They eat like gannets.
• On Cape Sable Island, Nova Scotia, folks so describe greedy eaters, people who bolt their food whole, as gannets swallow fish whole.

62. IDENTIFICATION

1. I don't know him from Adam's off ox.
• The off ox was the one in the barn, the ox not being used to plough on a specific day, when the job did not need a team of oxen.
•Monica Allison of Winnipeg reports her mother-in-law's phrase of puzzlement.

2. I'd know you if I saw a piece of your arse on a thorn bush in Ireland.

63. IFS, ANDS, AND BUTS

1. Yeah, and if my aunt had nuts, she'd be my uncle.
• Come-back when listener hears too many maybes during an argument or discussion.
From Nova Scotia.

64. ILLNESS

1. She was sick in bed on two chairs with her feet in the oven.
• Dorothy MacNeill of Truro, Nova Scotia, recalls her mother's expression in Newfoundland offered to children with a slight cold, to exemplify what someone really ill might have to endure.

2. How've you been? Up and down like a toilet seat at a sorority party.

3. I have a pain in my pinny.
• Said by a little girl complaining of a stomach ache. From turn-of-the-century days when little girls might have worn pinafores. A pinafore was a sleeveless, collarless overdress, worn over, say, a jumper or blouse. The pinafore was easily washable and was worn to protect clothes and keep some of the dirt off playing children. Naturally, no ship of Britain's Victorian navy would be named after a girl's dress, hence Gilbert and Sullivan's fun in their comic operetta *H.M.S. Pinafore*.

• Kate O'Donnell of Brantford remembers the expression of her great-grandmother who grew up in Waterford, Ontario.

4. His hemorrhoids stuck out like a bunch of grapes.

5. I feel like a dyin' calf in a hailstorm.
• This describes the onset of a bad cold in Vulcan, Alberta.

6. I feel like a pound of soap after a hard day's wash.

Heard in Oxford, Nova Scotia, in 1948, by Donald MacLean.

65. INCOMPETENCE

1. He couldn't hit a cow's arse with a grain scoop.
• Said perhaps of someone at bat in a baseball game.
Reino Kokkila, Etobicoke, Ontario

2. She couldn't drive sheep out of a garden.
Joe Wall, Grand Falls, Newfoundland

3. If he fell into a barrel of cunts, he'd come up holding his dick.
• A Newfoundland sailor's salty comment on some stumblebum deckhand.

4. He just can't gear down on the hills.
• He can't handle a situation requiring any intelligence.
Eleanor Hill, Calgary, Alberta

5. He couldn't drive a flax seed up a sow's ass with a trip hammer.
Ken Danchuk, Edmonton, Alberta

6. He couldn't drive a pea up a sow's ass with a frying pan.

66. INCREDULITY

1. In a pig's ass!
• This is a common North American expression of doubt in what a speaker is saying.
   Dolores Grant, Abbotsford, British Columbia

2. Do you see green in my eye?
• Do I look as gullible as a greenhorn?
   William Norman, London, Ontario

3. Well, smear my ears with jelly and tie me to a fence post!
   Becky Jo Baltimore, Edmonton, Alberta

4. That's more bubblegum than I can chew.

67. INTELLIGENCE

1. You're as bright as moonlight on a tin outhouse.

2. I didn't fall off a turnip truck.
• That is, I'm quite bright and not a hick.
   Reino Kokkila, Etobicoke, Ontario

3. He didn't just roll into town on a head of lettuce.

68. KNOW-IT-ALLS

1. He'd try to teach his grandmother how to suck eggs.

2. He knows as much about that as a dog knows about its grandmother.

Wilhelmine Estabrook, Hartland, New Brunswick

3. If you pull out a hanky, he'll tell you how to blow your nose.

Charlie Corkum, Summerside, P.E.I.

4. If your foresight was as good as your hindsight, you'd be too smart by a damn sight.

Diane Lowens Adam, Etobicoke, Ontario

69. LAZINESS

1. She's so lazy, you'd have to put a stake beside her to see if she's moving.

Marjorie Andrews, Bethany, Ontario

2. Advice to the lazy: Donkeys go best loaded.

3. He could work all day in a bushel basket and still have room to move.

4. *Avoir les deux pieds dans la même bottine.* 'To have both feet in one boot.'
• That is, to be lazy, to have no get-up-and-go.

5. Lazy as a red dog on a summer's day.

Beth Workman, Thunder Bay, Ontario

6. She'd roll over if it wasn't so much like work.
• Said of a lazy cat, by the father of Neil Simpson, Peterborough, Ontario.

7. Lazy as a pet coon.
• Raccoons kept as pets don't forage as much as they have to in the wild.

8. He's so lazy, a drop of his sweat would poison a snake.
• Presumably the lazy person has not sweated for so long that the concentration of impurities in his perspiration would zap an asp.

9. Likes work so much, he could sit and watch it all day.

Charlie Corkum, Summerside, P.E.I.

10. Just sittin' there, like a fly on a fresh turd.

11. She'll never drown in sweat.

70. LONELINESS

1. Lonely as a gander at settin' time.
• When female geese are incubating their eggs, they have no time for anserine hanky-panky.

71. LOST AND FOUND

1. It's up in Annie's room.

2. It's up Shaw's ass, picking raspberries.
• When seeking a misplaced item. British.

Tracy Carignan, Trenton, Ontario

3. It's down cellar behind the axe.
• Said when asked where something is. The answer implies equanimity: I don't know where it is, and I don't much care. Find it yourself.

72. LIARS

1. Reads like a Bre-X prospectus.
• Topical synonym for "a pack of lies," this was first said about a suspiciously worded document by Preston Manning during the federal spring election of 1997. Bre-X Minerals Incorporated owned an Indonesian gold mine near Busang, which company officials claimed held the largest reserve of gold known in the world. But it was alleged that ore samples had been altered and made to appear more gold-bearing than they were, after which Bre-X collapsed and Busang was declared a fraud. Hundreds of Canadians who had invested in the company lost money.

2. Your butt is suckin' wind!
• Said of a liar in Alberta.

3. If bullshit were a whistle, he'd be a brass band.

4. If bullshit were bullets, he'd be an arsenal.

5. Crookeder than a pan of guts.

6. It's a cake of lies with bullshit icing.

7. You are replete with an overabundance of a common fertilizer.

8. You're so full of it, your neck is brown.

9. "You're a liar," said the dummy; and the man with no legs got up and walked away.

10. You lie like a dirty rug.

11. Children's rhyme: "Liar, liar, pants on fire; nose as long as a telephone wire."

Dr. Brad Houston, Penticton, British Columbia

12. He's shitting, and his pants aren't even down yet.

13. I need an ear scoop to filter out the horse manure.

14. His mouth is so near his arse, his breath has a telltale odour.

73. MACHISMO

1. Back when men were men, and sheep were nervous.

2. With him, every night was like hormone day at the mink ranch.

3. I've got such a hard-on, a monkey couldn't climb it with cork boots.

4. I coughed up a jag big enough to knock up a cow.
• A jag is a small load, in this case, either of semen or phlegm.

5. Don't knock a guy for trying. That's all any steer can do.
• A reminder to the unin*farm*ed: a steer is a male bovine animal castrated before it attains sexual maturity.

Vivian Hansen, Calgary, Alberta

6. You'll be a man among geese when the gander's gone.
• Said to any bragging male.

7. He'll be a man before his mother.

8. He'd bang a snake if somebody'd hold its hips.

9. He's got a nine-inch prick, a twelve-inch tongue, and he can breathe through his ears.

10. He's so macho, he takes a wrench and loosens his nuts every night so he can get to sleep.

74. MENSTRUATION

1. The dam's up on the Red River.

2. Rosie's visiting.

3. The captain is at home.
• This euphemism for menses is first recorded in Britain in the 18th century, so it may be a pun on an early and now obsolescent medical term for menstruation, *catamenia*. It is worth noting how many synonyms for menses used by women refer to masculine names. I have heard the following: "Fred's here" and "This is Ben's week."

4. O.T.R.
• Acronym for "on the rag."

5. Riding the cotton bicycle.

6. To have the D.A.s
• Domestic afflictions.

7. The padlock's on the pleasure-garden.

8. The manhole cover's on.

9. To have (an attack of) the vapours.
• This Victorian euphemism for "the monthlies" was heard all across Canada until well into the late 1940s.

75. MESSINESS

1. It's a shithouse in distress.
• This Nova Scotian saying describes a very messy place.

2. A blind man would be glad to see it.
• Said of a messy job.
   Derwyn Evans, London, Ontario

3. Hit like shit from a tall cow in springtime.
   George Hart, Creemore, Ontario

4. Close the cupboard door. It's not an asshole. It doesn't close itself.
   Heard in French in Timmins, Ontario.

5. That house is so dirty, you wipe your feet leaving.
   Charlie Corkum, Summerside, P.E.I.

76. MILITARY SLANG

1. I shot better men than you for a dollar-fifty a day.
• World War II veteran's judgment of certain persons he met upon returning to Canada after the war.
   Linda Olson, Gimli, Manitoba

2. To pull a Mussolini.
• To stick your chin out when quickly putting on a gas mask. Late 1930s army camp and WWII phrase.
   William Norman, London, Ontario

3. I was in the army before Christ wore puttees.
• WWI slang. Puttees were cloth strips wrapped around the leg from the ankle to the knee for insulation.

They were introduced into Western military fashion
by the British army in 19th-century India, from the
Hindi word *patti* 'strip of cloth.'

4. To pull pole.
• Canadian army term meaning to take down your tent
on winter bivouac.

William Norman, London, Ontario

5. Don't look down; you'd find the hole soon enough
if there was hair around it!
• A Canadian army drill-instructor's command to
recruits learning to fix their bayonets without casting
a downward glance.

77. MISCELLANY
*This is my CATCH-ALL group of sayings that were
not put into other categories.*

1. He doesn't have his stick on the ice.
• He is not paying attention.

Carl Jansen, Saskatoon, Saskatchewan

2. About as flexible as a mile of CN rail.

Stephen Molloy, Winnipeg

3. Rough as a corduroy road.
• Pretty bumpy, like some Canadian pioneer roads
made of logs laid transversely across a roadbed.

4. Long as a sleigh track.
• This Canadian simile has regional variants such as
one from P.E.I.: "as straight as a sleigh track on the
Western Road," quoted in Pratt's *Dictionary of Prince
Edward Island English*.

5. You don't need that, any more than a cat needs side pockets.

Mary McLachlin, Toronto

6. Trust in Allah, but tie your camel securely.

7. Truckers' slang: Keep the steel side up, and the rubber side down.

8. There are more piglets than teats on the sow.
• Of people asking the government for funding.

9. I haven't seen you since Christ kicked the slats out of his cradle.

George Fairfield, Toronto, Ontario

10. Keep all your chairs at home.
• That is, mind your own business.

C. Ray, Sault Ste. Marie, Ontario

11. All ready but get ready.
• Prepared to depart with the briefest of preparations, for example, throwing on a hat and coat. Irish.

C. Ray, Sault Ste. Marie, Ontario

12. If it was a dog, you would have been et (eaten).

13. Don't poison your own well.

Jean Day, Sarnia, Ontario

14. No one just *has* spare time. When you need some, find it or make it.

LaVerne Higgs, Campbellford, Ontario

15. Jealous as two undertakers in a one-hearse town.

16. Subtle as hollyhocks around an outhouse.

17. Smooth as a butterfly's belly.

18. Said of a confined space: You could turn around and see yourself coming.

Mabell Parker, Port Coquitlam, British Columbia

19. As out of place as a brass doorknob on a pig pen.

Heard around Irma, Alberta.

20. He is the devil's lamp rag.
• This is said of a practical joker in Newfoundland.

Loretta Sherren, Fredericton, New Brunswick

21. A woman drives like a goose shits, in bunches.
• That is, women speed up, then slow down, then speed up again. A totally false and sexist generalization, and one that overlooks women's superior safety record as drivers.

22. Rebuke to a nitpicker: Have you ever been cut with a chainsaw and wondered which tooth did the cutting?

23. That's about as exciting as an Arborite dinette set.
• Arborite is a Canadian invention and was widely used in various kitchen-counter tops and table tops.

Fanny Keefer, Vancouver

24. To wait until the last dog's hung.
• This Canadian saying is explained by the late novelist Robertson Davies in one of his works of fiction. Davies says the Mohawk people held a Feast of the White Dog. They roasted and ate dogs, and the last dog to be hung and eaten was a white dog. No "reveller could leave the feast until the last white dog was hung."

Marilyn Browning, Gibsons, British Columbia

78. NERVOUSNESS

1. Up and down like a toilet seat on Fair Day.
John and Moira Elsley, Manitoulin Island, Ontario

2. Flittin' around like a blue-arsed fly on a thorn bush.
From Pictou County, Nova Scotia

3. Wired up like a Christmas tree.

79. NITPICKING

1. A blind man on a galloping horse would never notice it.

2. She'd look for a knot in a bulrush.
• She looks for problems where none exist.

3. Rebuke to a nitpicker: Ever been slashed with a chainsaw, and wondered which tooth did the cutting?

80. OBSESSIVE BEHAVIOUR

1. You don't know the difference between scratching your ass and tearing the skin off.
Kent Stetson, Halifax

2. He was toilet-trained at gunpoint.
• Said of obsessive-compulsive behaviour or of an anal-retentive personality.

81. OLD AGE

1. So old he could have been a waiter at the Last Supper.

2.

They'll never comb grey hair together.
• Said of a newly married couple who fight on their wedding day.

3. There's many a good tune played on an old fiddle.

4. You know you're gettin' up there, when your back goes out more than you do.

5. He's older than dirt.

6. He's two years older than God.

7. Don't pull a granny. Don't do a granny.
• This accuses the listener of shamming a hearing or memory loss.

   Colleen Saunders, Norman Wells, Northwest Territories

8. I had a brain fart.
• That is, the words were on the tip of my tongue, but I forgot.

9. As old as water.
• Maritime variant of "old as dirt."

10. I'm as old as my tongue and a little older than my teeth.
• This is one playful answer when a child asks an elder his or her age.

   Merrilee Ashworth, West Vancouver, British Columbia

11. There may be snow on the roof, but there is still fire in the furnace.

   Donald Fletcher, Nepean, Ontario

12. I have so many wrinkles, I can screw on my hat.
   Colleen Farrell, Head of Chezzetcook, Nova Scotia

13. Mutton dressed as lamb.
• Said of an overly made-up older woman.

Reino Kokkila, Etobicoke, Ontario

14. Old as the hills of Gowrie.
• This expression is still heard on Cape Breton Island. Gowrie is a town in Scotland.

82. OLD JOKES

1. First time I heard that one, I laughed so hard, I kicked a slat off my crib.

83. PATIENCE

1. Patience is a virtue. With the aid of vaseline, you can bugger a fly.

2. Variant of 1: With a little persistence and sweet oil, one could bugger a cat.

Derwyn Evans, London, Ontario

3. Patience is trying to take a pin out of your butt with a boxing glove.

84. PETS

1. That's a drop-kick dog.
• Said of teeny, yappy lapdogs which might serve better as footballs than as family pets.

Susan Jorgenson, Brampton, Ontario

2. It's a cross between a bull-bitch and a window shutter.
• Said when unable to identify a breed of dog.

Dona Crump, Regina, Saskatchewan

3. It's a waste of hair.
• Said of any pet dog or cat judged useless by an onlooker.

85. POSTURE

1. He was sitting up straighter than a tin god in an alder swamp.

Deborah Surette, Parrsboro, Nova Scotia

2. Hunched over like a skunk eating potato bugs.

From Chapleau in Northern Ontario.

86. POVERTY

1. Poor? We were so poor, if you didn't wake up in the morning with a hard-on, you had nothing to play with all day.
• Said by a well-known Canadian hockey star, speaking of his childhood in Western Canada. Also collected from Prince Edward Island as: So poor if we woke up Christmas morning without an erection, we had nothing to play with.

2. I'm so poor, I couldn't buy a louse a shootin' jacket.
• Paul Bell of Ontario writes, "When as a small child I asked for a penny for candy, my grandmother in Owen Sound used to say this."

3. His shoes were so thin, he could step on a dime and tell whether it was heads or tails.
• This is Depression-era humour from 1930s Saskatchewan.

4. I'm so poor, I couldn't buy a ticket to a free lunch.

5. Poor as Job's turkey. Couldn't raise more than three feathers, and had to lean against the barn to gobble.

6. They were so poor, there was nothing on the table but elbows, and the mice in the cellar had tears in their eyes.

7. He's poor because he invested all his money in houses and lots whorehouses and lots of booze.

   J.H. Toop, Windsor, Ontario

8. You'll find it mighty dry chewing.
• Advice to poor youngsters planning to get married and live on love.

9. *Arm wie a Kirchemaus.* 'Poor as a church mouse.'
• From the German of Mennonite and Amish farmers near Kitchener, Ontario (in standard German *arm wie eine Kirchenmaus*).

10. I'm so broke, I can't afford to pay attention.

11. Crime doesn't pay, and neither does farming.

12. He's so poor, he can't afford knee pants for a hummingbird.

13. He was always crying poor-mouth, like a farmer with a loaf of bread under each arm.

   Wilhelmine Estabrook, Hartland, New Brunswick

14. I've never been broke, just badly bent.

15. He'll always be farting through a thin pair of drawers.
• That is, he'll always be broke.

16. So poor they get their shoes half-soled one at a time.
Charlie Corkum, Summerside, P.E.I.

17. Every time I go into a store, my purse thinks my hands are crazy.
• From the Great Depression of the 1930s.

18. All they got ain't worth a pinch of coon shit.

19. I'm so broke, I'd have to buy a postage stamp on the installment plan.

20. When I was young, we never had shoes. We were so poor as kids, we just hopped from cow flop to cow flop.

87. QUIET

1. It was so quiet you could hear a fish fart.
John McGrath, Newfoundland

2. Quiet! There's a little boy dead in Lachine.
• Parent to noisy child in east Montreal, as remembered by Barry Evans of Pierrefonds, Québec.

3. It was so quiet, you could hear the fog lift.
From Newfoundland.

88. RARITY

1. Scarce as Pope-shit near a whorehouse.
• A bit of antipapal infrequency from Québec, where the original is *rare comme la merde de pape près d'un*

bordel. Merde is often pronounced 'marde' in *le français québécois.*

89. RCAF SLANG

1. During the Second World War, a common military gripe, heard even in the elite service of the Royal Canadian Air Force, was: "They treat us like mushrooms: keep us in the dark and feed us on horseshit."

2. Pay parade in the RCAF was "when the eagle shits."

3. I got more time in mess hall lineups than you got in the service.

4. If you can't take a joke, you shouldn't have joined up.

5. Warrant Officer: Are you in pain, private?
   Soldier: No, sir.
   WO: You should be. I'm standing on your goddamn hair!
• In other words: get a haircut.

6. WO to young recruit: Cut yourself next time, so I'll know you shaved.

7. WO to recruit with new moustache: Somebody hit you with a wet rope?

8. You can pass an armed forces medical "if you can see lightning and hear thunder."

9. Riggers and fitters wash before they piss; allied trades afterwards.

• In the RCAF, riggers and fitters handled airframes and engines, and the old piston engines were very dirty. Allied trades included electricians, instrument repairmen, radar technicians, etc.

Charlie Corkum, Summerside, P.E.I.

10. Parade square threat by drill sergeant, RCAF, 1944: "I shall piss upon you from the highest rafter in this building with deadly accuracy."

90. RELUCTANCE

1. He did it with long teeth.
• This expression existed in German long before it appears in English print, and so, it may be a loan-translation of *essen mit langen Zähnen,* 'to eat with long teeth.' John Finnie writes, "We have all experienced eating something that we do not like the taste of, and are familiar with the facial expressions grimaces of extreme reluctance that people make in such situations. It is as if one does not want to chew the food and thus tries to avoid the food even contacting the teeth. Consequently one does not bite deeply into the suspect food with relish, but instead nibbles at it, keeping it at the end of one's teeth, so to speak."

Kate O'Donnell, Brantford, Ontario, and John Finnie, Lantzville, British Columbia

91. REPUTATION

1. Earn the name of early riser, and you can sleep until noon.

92. RESOURCEFULNESS

1. We don't stretch our feet longer than our blankets.
• This is a Mennonite saying that's all about making-do with what one has been given.

2. There are more ways than one to skin a cat.

3. He'd sell an anchor to a drowning man.

4. He could fix the crack of dawn.

93. RESPONSIBILITY

1. If you burn your bum, you bear the blister.
• With its more widespread variant: "If you dance, you gotta pay the fiddler," itself an alteration of "who pays the fiddler, calls the tune" with its "money talks" echo.
A variant from Newfoundland: If you burns your ass, you sleeps on the blisters.

2. She paddles her own canoe.
• She is responsible for herself, an independent type who charts her own course.

3. She could sleep on a clothesline.
• Said of one who can rough it, or looks after herself responsibly.

4. He's apt to follow a team away.
• Wilhelmine Estabrook says this saying denotes an irresponsible type, like a bad watchdog on a farm that follows a team of horses down the lane.

94. RUNS IN THE FAMILY

1. You didn't lick that off the ground.

2. It wasn't from the grass he licked it.

3. She didn't get that from anybody strange.
• All these expressions mean that the person referred to is displaying a familial trait. The sayings came from Ireland.

4. Descended from a bull, a bitch, or a pine stump.
• Said of a person of uncertain lineage.

95. SADNESS

1. Sad enough to bring a tear to a glass eye.

2. There goes Gertie Gloom with a face longer than a daisy churn.

   Wilhelmine Estabrook, Hartland, New Brunswick

96. SEX & SEXIST SAYINGS
None of these sayings is politically correct, and many are revolting and offensive. All are nevertheless part of Canadian sexual speech. I would point out to those offended that anger and sexual insecurity play a large part in the habitual use of sexual put-downs. But I have not shied away from reporting this category of folk saying because it is part of common speech, and, because, frankly, the most offensive sexist sayings are often very funny, whether they refer to straight or gay sexual customs.

1. One male mocking the size of another male's penis:
I've seen chubbier clits.

2. I have sex regularly with the five sisters [speaker
holds up one hand].
• In our early West, this was a male's joking reference
to masturbation.

3. Woman to a man boasting of his sexual conquests:
I'm in no mood for an organ recital.

4. He's a real stud except that he couldn't get laid if he
were in a women's prison with a briefcase full of paroles.

5. *Grosse Corvette, p'tite quéquette.* 'Big car, little dick.'
• Said in Québec of an automotive braggart.

6. He was sowing his wild oats, but hoping for crop
failure.

7. When your cock stands up, your brain sits down.
• This paternal advice to a young man is a direct
translation from Yiddish.

8. Noisier than inbreeding on a cornhusk mattress.

9. With him, every night was like hormone day at a
mink ranch.

10. He's about as handy as a bear cub with its dick.
• Said of a sexually clumsy man.

11. He was on her like a chicken on a June bug.
  Geordie McConnell, Almonte, Ontario

12. He was all over her, like ugly on a gorilla.
  S. Rabbitte, Calgary, Alberta

13. He was all over her like white on rice.

14. You couldn't score in a fifty-cent whorehouse with a hundred-dollar bill.

15. He couldn't get laid in a whorehouse with a roll of fifty-dollar bills tied around his dick.
• A Newfoundland variant.

16. He fell for her like a blind roofer.
Heard in the Ottawa Valley by Geordie McConnell, Almonte, Ontario.

17. She's the town bicycle.
• Many men have ridden her.
Reino Kokkila, Etobicoke, Ontario

18. A stiff dick has no conscience.

19. She's showing more meat than a butchershop window.

20. There's not enough material in that to flag a train.
• Said of skimpy bikinis by a CNR engineer.

21. She's been married so many times, she's got veil rash.

22. Hotter than a flicker's nest.

23. She's been around, like a ring in a bathtub.

24. She's an all-weather gal. In the winter, use her to cuddle; in the summer, use her for shade.

25. That fellow's loose as a pan of soot.

26. Sincere as a chorus girl's kiss.

27. Whatever turns your crank.

28. *Devenir orignal.* 'To get horny.'
• Literally 'to become the moose.'

29. She was pure as the snow, but she drifted.

30. She's so butch, she kick-starts her vibrator and rolls her own tampons.

31. In the eastern townships of Ontario, a woman of loose morals was "the village mattress" and a similar man was "the town pump."

32. She's no better than she should be.

33. That dress is just about to eat her.

34. Bigamy is having one wife too many. Monogamy is the same thing.

35. A slice off a cut loaf is never missed.
• About enjoying the favours of a married woman.

36. A woman, a dog, and a walnut tree:
    The more you beat them, the better they be.
• An old Scottish rhyme brought over in the 19th century when abuse of women was wrongly celebrated in cheap verse.

37. Every pot finds its own cover.
• This is a direct translation from Dutch of a sexist thought sometimes expressed as "a girl for every boy."

38. Clark Harris of Moncton, New Brunswick, asked an old Nova Scotia fisherman about his lady friend and her honour. He replied, "Her honour! Yes, she offered her honour. I honoured her offer, and it was honour and offer all day long."

39. You're only as old as the woman you feel.

40. She could suck a golf ball through a garden hose.

41. She could suck the chrome off a bumper.

42. She's had more pricks than a second-hand dart board.

43. If she had as many sticking out of her as she'd had stuck in her, she could wrestle a porcupine and win.

44. If the Good Lord had given us three hands instead of a pecker, we would have been handier, but not happier.

45. I'm so horny, I could honk.
   Brian Lamarre, Ottawa, Ontario

46. I wouldn't say she's a whore, but she does douche with Janitor-in-a-Drum™ .

47. Your gay brother is like a grocery store. He takes meat in the back.

48. To a gay person in the closet: You're about as straight as a fever chart in a malaria ward.

49. He's hung like an animal — a tsetse fly.

50. She's like railway track. Been laid right across the country.

51. She's a biker's dream girl: 21 and can suck-start a Harley.

97. SHININESS

1. It's shining like shit on a barn door.
• Said of a newly washed car, floor, or a nice paint job.
   Tracy Carignan, Trenton, Ontario

83

98. SHYNESS

1. Wouldn't say boo to a goose.
• Old British expression, in print by A.D. 1580.

2. He wouldn't say baff to the shadow of a wolf.

99. SKEPTICISM

1. I'll tow her alongside awhile, before I bring her aboard.

From Nova Scotia.

2. I'd like to see a castor-oil painting of that.

Mabell Parker, Port Coquitlam, British Columbia

3. Let me run a swab on that, and I'll get back to you.
• From the Alberta oilfields, submitted by Ken Woadman of Calgary, this expression is also used by medical personnel in hospitals to indicate doubt about early diagnoses.

100. SLEEPING

1. If you don't get up soon, the sun is going to burn an extra hole in your ass.
• Said by a parent to slugabed children.

2. If you snooze, you lose.

Art Noble, Onoway, Alberta

3. I could stretch a mile away if I didn't have to walk back.

• From Apsley, Ontario, Pamela Miller remembers her mother saying this when rising from bed in the morning.

4. I guess it's time to climb the wooden hill.
• Going-to-bed line.
   LaVerne Higgs, Campbellford, Ontario.

5. When I was a young fella I could sleep on a clothesline in a windstorm.
   Denis Dohie, Russell, Manitoba

6. I'm going to throw up my feet and drop off.
• That is, I'm going to take a nap.
   Beth Workman, Thunder Bay, Ontario

7. He was so tired, he went to sleep in puppy's parlour.
• This Newfoundland expression means he fell asleep in his day clothes.
   Peter Chalker, St. John's, Newfoundland

8. You clung to the wreck a long time this morning.
• *You slept in* is the gist of this Nova Scotia saying.
   Peggy Devers, Comox, British Columbia

9. People die in bed, you know.
• Advice to children who don't want to get up in the morning.
   Dave Pauls, Saskatoon, Saskatchewan

10. When late sleepers finally get up: The dead arose and appeared to many.
   Ursula Wall, Grand Falls, Newfoundland

11. I'm so tired, I could sleep on a spike harrow.
   From Prince Edward Island.

12. I slept like a winter woodchuck.
   George Fairfield, Toronto

13. My mouth is as dry as a covered bridge.
• Upon waking after snoring all night.

Sandra Morrison, Bury, Québec

14. Call to children sleeping late: Get up! It's daylight in the swamp.
• That is, it is already late morning, the time by which daylight presumably has penetrated the dark gloom of a swamp.

Stan Hingston, Rosetown, Saskatchewan

101. SLIPPERINESS

1. Slippery as a greased eel tit.
• Said of road conditions after an ice storm or freezing rain.

Shirley MacMillan, West Covehead, P.E.I

2. Slick as a slut's tit.
• Kent Stetson points out that, in Prince Edward Island farm slang, a slut is a cow which has produced and calved well for many years.

3. Not slippery: as smooth as a stucco bathtub.

102. SMALL-MINDEDNESS

1. She's narrower than hen's eyes.

103. SMELLS & ODOURS

1. He's got breath like a buffalo fart.

• Linda Grasswick of Dalhousie University in Nova Scotia first heard this one near Ottawa from a native of our Prairies.

2. It smelled like the shithouse door off a tuna boat.

3. Two whiffs of that and you're a glutton.
• Said of any noxious odour.
  Peter Polley, North York, Ontario

4. Stench? That would drive a buzzard off a dead cow.

5. That smell would gag a maggot on a gut wagon.

6. Variant: So rotten it would drive a hound from a gut wagon.

7. You smell better than a dime whore on nickel Tuesday.
  Heard in Sault Ste. Marie, Ontario.

8. Go outside and blow the stink off you!
• E.C. Lougheed reminds us of this dead-of-winter advice from the days when there was no running water in a home, and men changed their long underwear infrequently.

9. 1st person: What are you smoking? Plank Road?
   2nd person: What's Plank Road?
   1st person: Horse manure and slivers.
• This interchange concerned cheap, pungent tobacco.

104. SNOBBERY

1. Margaret Reid of Dundas, Ontario, writes: "My grandmother used to say that a snooty or conceited

person was 'smelling thunder' (walking around with their nose in the air)."

2. *È s'mouche pas avec des pelures d'oignons.*
• In Québec slang, to indicate an uppity woman, one might say, "She wouldn't blow her nose on an onion peel."

3. He couldn't say shit if his mouth was full of it.

4. The higher the monkey climbs, the more he shows his arse.

5. He was wearing Full Nanaimo.
• Are B.C. recreational boaters and yachtsmen a trifle snooty? They seem to pay finicky attention to how their fellow mariners dress. Full Nanaimo is an insult that applies to a chintzy outfit worn by a boating parvenu. Whitebuck shoes, white belt, polyester pants, and a blue blazer with a spurious yachting crest brand the wearer as a floating yutz of the first water. In Ontario, it is heard as a Full Oakville. A similar chop is FDAM, pronounced to rhyme with ram. The acronym stands for **F**irst **D**ay **a**t the **M**arina.

6. She goes with her head up and her tail over the dashboard.
• That is, too proud by half.

7. You come of good blood and so does a black pudding.
• This is said to deflate one boasting of high birth. A black pudding was also called a blood pudding because of one ingredient.

8. They're very haw-haw.

• This was said early in the 20th century by Canadians about newly arrived immigrants from Britain who were putting on airs, pretending to be terribly upper class, don't you know. During World War II, a Nazi-sympathizer named William Joyce did radio broadcasts of anti-British propaganda from Germany. His plummy accent caused Fleet Street to dub him "Lord Haw-Haw." But Joyce wasn't laughing when he was hanged for treason in 1946.

105. SPORTS

1. Hit them with your hockey!
• This coach's advice to his players suggests that prowess rather than fists might win the game.

Rod Lisenchuk, Nanisivik, Northwest Territories

106. STINGINESS

1. He would fart on a stone to save the grease.
John A.D. McLean, Belleville, Ontario

2. Tighter than a frog's ass, and that's watertight.

3. He'd give you the sleeves off his vest.

4. Tighter than a wet boot.

5. She's so cheap she avoids cold showers, because goosebumps are hard on soap.

6. Money? Stuck to him like snot to a suede jacket.

7. He was so tight, you couldn't drive a flax seed up his ass with a mallet.

8. So cheap, he'd pick the pennies off a dead man's eyes, and then kick the corpse because they weren't quarters.

9. Tighter than a bull's arse in fly time.

10. She's so cheap, she'd skin a louse for the tallow.

11. He's so tight, when he farts, his ankles swell.

12. He's so stingy, he wouldn't pay a nickel to see Jesus go over Niagara Falls on water skis.

13. Variant: She's so cheap she wouldn't give ten cents to watch Christ ride an ATV (all-terrain vehicle).

14. She's so tight, she'd squeeze a cent until the Queen cried.

15. He's so cheap, he skims the lard off his farts.

16. She's so cheap, when she opens her purse, the Queen squints.

17. He's so cheap, he wouldn't give you the droppings of his nose.

18. She squeezes a nickel until the beaver shits.

19. He's tighter than a crofter's lease.
• This bitter line, almost always uttered in full earnest, was brought to Canada from the Scottish Highlands in the days of skinflint lairds and massive eviction of crofters, when it proved more profitable for absentee landlords to raise sheep than to let human beings eke out a miserable subsistence.

20. He's so tight, if you shoved a piece of coal up his ass, it would come out a diamond.

21. He's so tight, he wouldn't pay a dime to see a pismire eat a bale of hay.
• A pismire is an ant. This is cowboy Cliff Vandergrift's saying, reported by his friend Stan Gibson of Okotoks, Alberta.

22. He has his first dollar and half the arm of the man he got it off.

23. He's so tight, he squeaks when he walks.

24. So cheap, they wouldn't boil shit for a tramp.
   Ken Danchuk, Edmonton, Alberta

25. He's hard as the knockers of Newgate.
• Referring to the giant doors of a famous British prison.
   Janet Hingley, New Glasgow, New Bruswick

26. Tight as a fiddle string.

107. STRENGTH & TOUGHNESS

1. Harder than the back of God's head.
   Derwyn Evans, London, Ontario

2. So tough, you couldn't kill him with a sleigh stake.
• A sleigh stake is one of the pieces of 2 x 4 secured in the corner and centre brackets on a "horsedrawn sleigh that hauls loads such as logs that might fall off the sleigh without stakes."
   Charlie Corkum, Summerside, P.E.I.

3. Harder than the lips on a woodpecker.

4. She can eat sawdust and shit 2 x 4s.

5. Keep your ears stiff.
• A command to endure whatever befalls one, this is offered to ease sorrow even at a funeral.

Grace Johnson of Winnipeg heard this in Walkerton, Ontario.

6. He's tough as leather lightning.

108. STUPIDITY
Although all these expressions may indicate stupidity, many of them also denote various degrees of craziness, odd behaviour, or "suitable cases for treatment."

1. Hang crepe on your nose; your brains are dead.

2. You were born ignorant and you've been losing ground ever since.

3. He doesn't know which finger to scratch his nuts with.

4. It'll never get well if you pick it.

5. His elevator doesn't go all the way to the top.
Donald Smith, North Bay, Ontario

6. He's not the sharpest knife in the drawer.

7. He's about two sandwiches short of a picnic.

8. If brains were lard, he wouldn't grease much of a pan.

9. Two bricks short of a pallet.

10. He doesn't know "Sic him" from "Get out."
• Said of a dumb person or dog.

11. Stupid as the day is long.

12. He doesn't know enough to suck alum and drool.
• From the days of patent medicines, when alum powder was used as an expectorant.

13. One wall in his attic isn't plastered.

14. He couldn't pour piss out of a boot if the instructions were printed on the heel.
• This Canadian folk saying, widespread after the First World War, indicated lack of intelligence. The expression originated in 1915 when Canadian soldiers were issued new army boots made of stiff leather. Oddly enough, a legitimate method of softening leather is to urinate in the boots and leave it in overnight. Of course, it helps if one empties and washes the footwear in the morning, before attending to one's military duties.

15. He's stunned as Tom's dog — put his arse in the water to get a drink.

16. If brains were leather, you wouldn't have enough to make spats for a louse.

17. I've seen more brains in a sucked egg.

18. No use keepin' a dog and barkin' yourself.

19. He's got his solar panels on the north side.
Ron Bronson, Waterloo, Ontario

20. Number than a hake.

21. Bright as a two-watt bulb.

22. Dull as a box of dirt.

23. He has a one-track mind, and that's narrow gauge.
• An old Canadian railroader's insult.
  J.H. Toop, Windsor, Ontario

24. She's nine parts damn fool.

25. He's so stupid, he thinks Medicine Hat is a cure for head lice.

26. He's got rooms for rent upstairs.
• This saying has a British equivalent: "He's an apartment to let."

27. I see shells; I can guess eggs.
• This implies the speaker is not stupid.
  From P.E.I.

28. Talking to him is like pissing in the wind and trying not to get wet.
• That is, he's stupid, and so are you for trying to talk to him.

29. That explains the milk in the coconut.
• Said upon hearing an explanation of something complicated. This is a sly pretense of stupidity on the part of the speaker.

30. Were you born in a barn?
• Said to someone who foolishly leaves a door open.

31. Green as duckweed.
• Foolish, but approaching stupidity.

32. His driveway doesn't go all the way to the road.
  Bill Bowman of Selkirk, Manitoba, offers this variant:
His driveway don't go all the way to the garage.

33. There'a a wet wire in his fuse box.

34. The wheel is spinning, but the hamster is dead.

35. He doesn't know if his asshole was punched, bored, or burnt out by lightning.

36. Sharp as a beach ball.

37. His intake manifold is sucking air.
   Brian Burnett, Lindsay, Ontario

38. He's not firing on all eight cylinders.

39. Just as happy as if he had brains, isn't he?
• Theresa Lemieux reports her Irish grandmother's favourite put-down.

40. He's two potatoes short of a bushel.
   Betty and Bob Romkey, Petite Rivière, Nova Scotia

41. She's not the brightest star in heaven.
Joan Walsh heard this during her youth in Nova Scotia.

42. He needs his attic rewired.

43. Got a mind like a squid.

44. You are stunned as stump.

45. Not too bright in Toronto: Strong like bull, dumb like streetcar.

46. A few floats short of a parade.

47. A few stitches short of a tapestry.

48. A few dollars short of a haircut.

49. A few colours short of a rainbow.

50. A few boards short of a bookcase.

51. A few jewels short of a crown.

52. A few countries short of an empire.

53. A few pitches short of an inning.

54. A few items short of a menu.

55. A few camels short of a caravan.

56. A few brush strokes short of a painting.

57. A few tomatoes short of a sauce.

58. A few tiles short of mah-jongg.

59. A few buckets short of a fire brigade.

60. A few dunes short of a desert.

61. A few cogs short of a gear.

62. His river doesn't run all the way to the sea.

63. His engine is running, but it's still in neutral.

64. His porch light is on, but the wattage is dim.
   Items 46 to 64 contributed by Tracy Carignan, Trenton, Ontario.

65. Tall like a poplar; stupid like a bean.
• This Canadian Prairie put-down is a direct translation from Ukrainian: *visocki yak polya; dorni yak fasolya* [rough transliteration].

   Thanks to Theresa Zolner.

66. That boy doesn't know whether to shit or steal third.
• A metaphor drawn from baseball.

   Clay and Wendy Nairn.

67. He doesn't know *a lot* about sports. He thinks a quarterback is change from a dollar.

   Dave Ferguson, Scarborough, Ontario

68. He forgot to install the pump on the skunk.
• Marcel Lemoine of Winnipeg sends this delightful comment on someone either forgetful or stupid or both.

69. He's one buttress short of a cathedral.

Harry King, Edmonton, Alberta

70. He only has one oar in the water.

71. He has his thumb up his bum and his mind in neutral.

David Ruddy, Montreal, Québec

72. When you're up to your ass in alligators, it's too late to start figurin' out how to drain the swamp.
• J.W. Manson of Winnipeg, Manitoba, remembers this cogent bit of managerial wisdom from his days in a railway office.

73. You wouldn't know piss from paint.

74. He couldn't get a job as a village idiot with Einstein's résumé.

Michael Scott, Vancouver

75. You don't know if your ass is punched, bored, or burnt out in the Miramichi fire.

Lydia Cassidy, Taymouth, New Brunswick

76. He's got a couple of shingles missing, and the rain is getting in.

Stephen Molloy, Winnipeg

77. Family was so inbred, when one woman has a baby, they all give milk.

78. Bunch of inbred arsewipes with crossed, pink eyes. If any kid at the table cries, "Daddy!" all the men stand up.

79. If he had dynamite for brains, it wouldn't be enough to raise his hat.

Helen Forsyth, Gatineau, Québec

80. If brains were soap, he wouldn't have enough to lather a mosquito's eyeball.

Marlene Moore, Golden Valley, Ontario

81. So stupid, when you say hello, he's stuck for an answer.

82. If brains were vinegar, she wouldn't have enough to pickle an egg.

83. He's a few clowns short of a circus.

84. She's an experiment in artificial stupidity.

85. A few beers short of a six pack.

86. Dumber than a box of hair.

87. A few peas short of a casserole.

88. He doesn't have all his cornflakes in the same box.

89. One Fruit Loop™ "short of a full bowl."

90. All foam, no beer.

91. The cheese slid off his cracker.

92. Body by Fisher, brains by Mattel™.
• Fisher makes car chassis; Mattel™ makes toys.

93. Has an IQ of 2; but it takes 3 to grunt.

94. Sign for a stupid person's bathroom: Warning: Objects in mirror are dumber than they appear.

95. Too much yardage between the goalposts.

96. An intellect rivalled only by her garden tools.

97. Smart as bait.

98. The chimney's clogged.

99. He doesn't have all his dogs on the same leash.

100. She doesn't know much, but she leads her bowling league in nostril hair.

101. He forgot to pay his brain bill.

102. Her sewing machine's out of thread.

103. His antenna doesn't pick up all the channels.

104. His cable service is down permanently.

105. His belt doesn't go through all the loops.

106. She's missing a few buttons on her remote control.

107. There's no grain in that silo.

108. He's proof that evolution can go in reverse.

109. His receiver is off the hook.

110. He's several nuts short of a full pouch.

111. She doesn't know if she's washin' or hangin' out.

112. Alright. If he's not a dick-head, then what do you call someone with a foreskin for a neck?

113. Sharp as a marble.

114. If brains were ink, he wouldn't be able to dot an i.

115. He couldn't organize a piss-up at a brewery.

Ken Woadman, Calgary, Alberta

116. She's half a bubble off centre.
• From using a spirit level.

117. He was born on a raft.
• Said in New Brunswick of anyone ignorant of the social graces.

118. If shoes were clues, you'd be barefoot.
  Joe Wall, Grand Falls, Newfoundland

119. When the brains were being handed out, she went through the tit line twice.

120. Well, he didn't invent the four-hole button.
• Direct translation from Canadian French: *C'est pas lui qui a inventé les boutons à quatre trous.*

121. He's a few tiles short of a roof.
• Compare the Canadian French version: *Il lui manque des bardeaux.* 'He's missing a few tiles.'

122. He doesn't know if he was born or hatched.

123. His stairs don't go all the way to the top.

124. She's missing a few rungs in her ladder.

125. He's not playing with a full deck.

126. He's only got one oar in the water.

127. *C'est pas un 100 watt.*
• He's not a bright light.
  Alison Hackney, Senneville, Québec

128. All his dogs aren't barking.
  Susan Jorgenson, Brampton, Ontario

129. He's so dumb, he wouldn't know shit from wild

honey without tasting them both twice.

Ken Danchuk, Edmonton, Alberta

130. Thicker than a B.C. pine.

William Norman, London, Ontario

131. Gust o' wind musta blowed out his pilot light.

132. Her johnnycake isn't done in the middle.

133. He lost his ball in the rough and never found it.

134. Her lid's on too tight.

135. He's dead from the arse both ways.
• An expression indicating both dullness and lethargy.
• From Dundas County, Ontario, heard as a child by my father, Alfred M. Casselman.

109. SURPRISE

1. Wouldn't that give your tuque a spin.

2. There he stood, winkin' and blinkin' like a toad under a spike-toothed harrow.

From Aylesford, Nova Scotia

• Did Rudyard Kipling hear this expression in England, or, is the expression an echo of Kipling's lines from *Departmental Ditties* (1886):

The toad beneath the harrow knows,
Exactly where each tooth point goes;
The butterfly upon the road
Preaches contentment to that toad.

Thanks for finding that quotation to Peggy Feltmate of Toronto.

3. If that don't bang all!

4. I've been around the Horn.
• That is, nothing surprises me; I've had plenty of experience in life, the equivalent of sailing around Cape Horn.

5. Well, shit and fall back on it!

6. Now wouldn't that just jar your preserves!

Phyllis Roussie, Campbellton, New Brunswick, and Guy Charbonneau, Timmins, Ontario, sent variants like:

Wouldn't that jar your mother's preserves.

7. Gross me green, and call me Kermit.
• This expression from Neil's Harbour, Nova Scotia, refers to the green frog puppet Kermit, created by Jim Henson, originally for TV's *Sesame Street*.

8. Wouldn't that physic a snipe!
• Dona Crump, of Regina, Saskatchewan, contributed her father's favourite expression of surprise.

9. Wouldn't that just frost your liver.
• Widespread saying, contributed by Siri McCormick, a favourite of her mom who grew up in Battrum, Saskatchewan.

110. TEA

1. The tea is strong enough to trot a mouse on.
• This phrase indicates the point at which certain English persons think tea has been brewed to sufficient potency and is fit to drink.

Contributed by Peter Polley, a teacher at York Mills Collegiate Institute in North York, who picked it up from his English grandmother.

2. That tea is so weak, it comes out of the pot on crutches.

From the Feltmate family of Guysborough County in Nova Scotia.

3. Tea strong enough to float an iron wedge.

Marguerite Hill, Barrie, Ontario

4. Of weak tea: It's just water bewitched and tea bedamned.

111. TEETH CHIEFLY BUCKED

1. Whole family's got buck teeth. Great-grandfather musta jumped a beaver.

2. Buck teeth? She could eat an apple through a tennis racquet.

3. Buck teeth? Only man I ever met could eat grass through a picket fence.

4. Buck teeth? Only guy I ever saw could eat a tomato through a tennis racquet.

5. He had a set of teeth, would make a bucksaw sing with envy.

6. She looks like she could eat oats from the bottom of a pop bottle.

Ken Danchuk, Edmonton, Alberta

7. He could eat through a Venetian blind.

112. TENACITY

1. Holding on like a puppy to a root.

2. Perserverance: Every shot is a potential goal.
• In hockey, as in life.
  Grant Toll, Nepean, Ontario

113. THEFT

1. It's okay to steal from the government or the CPR. It was probably yours in the first place.

2. Might as well be shot for a sheep as a lamb.
  Jean Gibson, Thunder Bay, Ontario

3. He'd steal a soggy doughnut out of a bucket of snot.

114. THINGAMAJIGS

1. I had one but the wheels fell off.
• Said when asked about an object of which one is ignorant.

2. A silver know-nothing with a whistle on top.
• When elders are asked by children what they want for Christmas, the adult gives this reply.

3. Handy as a pocket on a shirt.
• Said of a clever, new device.

4. What is it? It's a hoojar kapiv.
• If *hoojar kapiv* is a foreign phrase for a whatchamacallit, I could not discover it, and would appreciateit if any reader can identify its language and literal meaning.

5. What is it? It's a silver-handled yoodel-addel-um for pumping cold piss out of a dead cat.

Kent Stetson, Halifax.

6. When not able to report an illness by its correct medical term: She's got collywobbles of the diaphloric colorum.
• According to Keith Bird of Viscount, Saskatchewan, this nonsense phrase was also used to answer children who asked about women in late pregnancy.

115. THINKING

1. That girl's bright as a head of cabbage in a pumpkin field.

2. *Être une tête à Papineau.* 'To be a Papineau head.'
• This *québécois* folk saying that means to be very clever recalls one of the heroes of French-Canadian history. Joseph Louis Papineau (1786-1871) led a group of radical reformers in Lower Canada. Their grievances against the government of the day came to a head in the Rebellion of 1837, fomented by Papineau in Lower Canada, and William Lyon Mackenzie in Upper Canada.

3. *Vous vous faites aller la marde de tête.*
• You are concentrating really hard. Literally 'You are going to pass a brain turd.'

116. THINNESS

1. She hasn't enough ass on her to keep your balls out of the sand.

2. He's so thin his pyjamas only got one stripe.

3. He's so skinny, if he took a dose of salts, why, we could watch it work.

4. She's so thin, she has to run around the shower to get wet.

5. He's so thin, he has to stand in the same place twice, just to make a good shadow.

6. Of a very thin bride: Poor dear, she's so thin he'll have to shake the sheets to find her on their wedding night.

7. He's so thin, if he drank a glass of tomato juice, he'd look like a thermometer.

Charlie Corkum, Summerside, P.E.I.

8. Thin? I've seen more meat on a hockey stick.

9. More meat on a butcher's pencil.

Ivan and Janet Beedom, St. Williams, Ontario

10. He's finer than frog hair.
• But this expression is also used to indicate good health.

11. He was so thin, you could count his teeth with his mouth closed.

Beverly Newmarch, Calgary, Alberta

12. It'd be like screwing a sackful of moose antlers.
• Said in sexual contemplation of a skinny woman: This is a Métis expression, translated from Cree.

Contributed by Blaine Klippenstein of Sherridon, Manitoba.

13. So skinny she hasn't enough flesh to pad a crutch.

• Heard in Newfoundland and Nova Scotia.
David J. Thomas

14. Thin as the rames.
• An old Newfoundland expression, rames are bones or a skeleton. The singular, rame, meaning 'a bone,' is obsolete in current English, except in some dialects. It is a Germanic root related to *Rahm* 'frame' and *Rahmen* 'framework' in German, and perhaps borrowed into English first through its Dutch cognate *raam*, the idea being that the framework of the body is its skeleton. In Newfoundland, rames are also, according to the *Dictionary of Newfoundland English*, "the keel and ribs of a boat or vessel, derelict on the shore." Someone thin as a skeleton is ramey.

15. I've seen more meat on Good Friday.

16. Of one who is tall and thin: If she stood sideways and stuck out her tongue, she'd look like a zipper.

17. Just like an Indian dog, all ribs and nuts.
• This offensive simile was heard long ago near Edmonton, Alberta.

18. No more worth fucking than a robin's arse.
Heard in southern Ontario.

117. THREATS

1. Cruisin' for a bruisin'.
• Once in high school gym class I asked the phys. ed. teacher about the value to my intellectual development of vaulting repeatedly over a gym horse. I

received the reply, "Casselman, you're cruisin' for a bruisin'." Herewith some alternative bullyings that yahoos may wish to caterwaul at underlings:

2. Achin' for a breakin'.

3. Aimin' for a maimin'.

4. Hurtin' for certain.

5. Do it again, and I'll slap you bald-headed.

6. I'll hit you so hard, you'll starve to death bouncin'.

7. I'll pull a leg off you and spank you with it.

8. I'll give you what Paddy gave the drum.
• Namely, a damn good beating. Possibly of Irish origin.

9. I'll hit you so hard, when you wake up, your clothes will be out of style.

10. I'll beat you like a rented mule.

Deidra Grisdale, Weekes, Saskatchewan

11. I'll smack you so hard, you'll land in the middle of next week.

Geoff Adams, Milton, Trinity Bay, Newfoundland

12. Do that again, and you'll wish the pigs had eaten you when you were little.

Lorna MacKenzie, Petawawa, Ontario

13. I'll have your guts for garters.

Reino Kokkila, Etobicoke, Ontario

14. I'll kick the slats off you.
• Heard by my father, Alfred Merkley Casselman, in his youth near Williamsburg, Dundas County, Ontario.

An infant might kick the slats off a turn-of-the-century crib, or a farmer might kick the slats off the side of certain farm wagons before loading or unloading them.

15. I'll knock you into next week.

16. I'll hit you so hard, your kids'll be born dumb.

17. You're askin' for a pine box.

18. I'm gonna snatch you bald-headed.

118. TOOLS & IMPLEMENTS

1. That blade is so dull you could ride bare-assed to Halifax on it.
A variant: You could ride to Halifax on that blade.
• This workaday saying is still heard in Eastern Canada, referring to a dull knife, a scythe, or other bladed implement.

2. Like the preacher's finger in kitty's arsehole, it fits where it touches, and it's close all round.
• This is carpenters' slang for well-done woodwork.
  George Hart, Creemore, Ontario

3. On driving skills: I've got more miles in reverse than you've got going forward.
  Joe Wall, Grand Falls, Newfoundland

4. Handy? Guy could sew a canvas arse into a dog.
• A Nova Scotian expression.

5. He could put a wooden arse on a cat.
• Said of someone who is handy. Variant of 4.

6. That water pump is as noisy as seven devils and twice the trouble.

Arthur Rhynold, Guysborough County, Nova Scotia

7. I cut that board off three times and it's still too short.
• Comic complaint of a carpenter.

8. Of a dim miner's lamp: It shows about as much light as a white bean up a black cat's ass.

9. Of contact cement: So strong, it would stick a bulldozer to a rainbow.

Charlie Corkum, Summerside, P.E.I.

10. He doesn't know a whiffletree from a neck yoke.
• He is not acquainted with the parts of a wagon, or by implication, with farm work in general. When horses or oxen, often in teams of two, are used to pull wagons and sleighs, a whiffletree is the pivoted bar to which the traces of a harness are fastened. The whiffletree attaches to the back end of the tongue or pole of a wagon by means of a clevis. A neck yoke attaches to the hames, the two curved pieces of wood or iron that form part of the collar of a draught horse. This yoke has a ring in its centre through which the end of the wagon tongue protrudes. A neck yoke serves to change the direction of the wagon. Since the whiffletree and the neck yoke were used at opposite ends of a draught horse, the expression was used humorously to indicate that someone didn't know one end of the horse from the other.

Submission and explanation by Douglas F. Edwards, Ottawa.

11. That's a haywire fix.

• A 1930s expression indicating a temporary and not very reliable repair. Haywire was used to repair as many things as possible on a poor farm, as much later we speak of Band-Aids "or duct tape."

Dr. Brad Houston, Penticton, British Columbia

12. Of mechanical problems: "That's stuck in tighter than snot up a rooster's beak."

13. He could fix the crack of dawn.

119. UGLINESS

1. Ugly? Looks like a dog's arse sewn up with a logging chain.

Teresa Sinkowski, Waterford, Ontario

2. Ugly as a bouquet of smashed assholes.

3. Variant of 2: Homely as a cartload of fannies.

4. Uglier than forty acres of burning stumps.

From Northumberland County, Ontario.

5. She fell out of the ugly tree, and on the way down hit every branch.

6. Homely as a hedge fence.

Carol Aubé, Barrie, Ontario

7. Got a face like a ripple in a swill bucket.

8. He's so ugly that, when he was born, the doctor slapped his mother.

9. *Laid comme un pichou.*

• *Pichou*, 'lynx' in Québec French, also means the soft

grey moccasins used with snowshoes. A face looking like a blackened, oft-wetted and dried *pichou* would qualify as ugly.

Jean Paré, Outremont, Québec

10. He's so ugly he has to slap his feet to make them go to bed with him.

11. She looked like a professional blind date.

12. She was ugly when I met her in the beverage room, but I drank her pretty.

13. He's so ugly, when he looks in a mirror, it fogs itself over.

14. He looks like the back of a hack.
• The backboards of a hackney coach were often mud-spattered from the unpaved streets of the 19th century and frequently bedaubed with horse manure.

15. If I had a face like that, I'd shave my ass and walk backwards.

16. I could shave my dog's arse and teach it to walk backwards, and still look better than you.

17. Ugly? Looks like he came third in an axe fight.

From Red Deer, Alberta.

18. She was so ugly, she got a job as a test pilot in a broom factory.
• Ann-Marie Leblanc of London, Ontario, remembers this saying of her Nova Scotian father.

19. He's uglier than a hairpin-turn at a rototiller race.
• Shelly Goldsack heard this from a native of Calihoo, Alberta.

20. She's as plain as pauper's pudding.

21. He's as handsome as the south end of a northbound cow.

22. She was so ugly, her mother had to tie a porkchop around her neck to get the dog to play with her.

Wendy Griswold, Edmonton, Alberta

23. He's got a face only a mother could love on payday.

From Linda Grasswick at Dalhousie University.

24. Ugly as last year's valentine.

25. She looks like the skin of a nightmare pulled over a broom handle.

26. He had a face that would make an onion cry.

27. He's so ugly, he'd make a train take a dirt road.

28. His eyes bug out like a choked rat's ass.
• This unkindness perhaps labelled a victim of exophthalmic goitre in days gone by.

29. My, what an ugly child! Guess that's why his mother sets him in the corner and feeds him with a slingshot.

30. I know you can't help being ugly, but you could stay home.

31. Her face might not stop a clock, but it would sure raise hell with small watches.

32. What do you charge to haunt a house?

120. UNPLEASANTNESS

1. Don't change. I want to forget you as you are.

2. She's a hurricane on a ten-cent piece.

3. Livin' with him's about as much fun as having a shit hemorrhage in a hurricane.
• Medical literature is silent about the dread malady here christened 'shit hemorrhage' which I first heard in my native Ontario county of Haldimand. But folk descriptions of infectious mishaps often have their own humour. Doreen Andreson writes to tell me about the old fellow in rural Manitoba who didn't have much education, but was just as concerned as you or I would be after a visit to his physician: "Doc says I got the diarrhea in my teeth, and it went all down through my cistern."

4. Meaner than a junkyard dog with fourteen suckin' pups.

5. He's enough to make a saint swear.

6. He's slicker than deer guts on a doorknob.
• Bill Bowman of Selkirk, Manitoba, writes that this expression was a favourite of his father-in-law, a bush pilot who retired to run a trapline in eastern Manitoba.

7. He's rough as a sea-dog's back.

8. Colder than a Bay Street banker's heart.

9. I could have shot him for a bear.
• Said of a disagreeable person.
  Derwyn Evans, London, Ontario

10. He's an orbicular S.O.B.
• From RCAF slang, he's a son-of-a-bitch who's well

rounded. Or, he's a son-of-a-bitch no matter which way you look at him.

Charlie Corkum, Summerside, P.E.I.

11. Cutting a dog's tail off by inches, so it won't hurt as much.
• Being nasty frequently but at brief intervals is still being nasty.

Kate O'Donnell, Brantford, Ontario

121. UNTIDINESS

1. He looks like he threw his clothes in the air, and ran under them.

2. She looks like she just spent a month in her 18-hour bra.

3. She dresses like a sow with side pockets.

4. Dressed up like a sore finger.

5. Looks like he's been chewin' tobacco and spittin' downwind.

6. You could eat off her kitchen floor. Piece of cake here, slice of bread there.

122. VOMITING

1. To make a call on the porcelain telephone.
• This is a synonym for vomiting into the toilet bowl.

2. To reconsider breakfast.
• This is an Ontario summer camp euphemism for the verb "to vomit."

3. To york.
• This has been playfully suggested as the perfect Toronto synonym for the verb "to vomit." Many of the synonyms for vomit arise from imitating the sound of vomition, e.g. barf, cack, puke, ralph, and retch.

4. To defood.
• A bit of euphemistic gobbledygook that nicely avoids the unpleasant nature of vomiting.

123. WAGERING

1. I'll kiss your ass at high noon right downtown and give you half an hour to draw a crowd.

124. WATER

1. Too wet to walk on, but too dry to drink.
• Saskatchewan water is sometimes described this way.

2. Too soft to walk on, but too hard to drink.
• Saskatchewan water in a dry year.
  Bob Miller, Regina, Saskatchewan

125. WEAKNESS

1. He's so weak, he couldn't dent a pound of butter.

2. Poor dear was so weak she couldn't pull the skin off a rice pudding.

3. He's so weak, he couldn't pull his finger out of a lard pail.

4. He's as harmless as a declawed kitten.

Andy van Esch, Sardis, British Columbia

5. I feel like I've been cow-kicked by a bowlegged bumblebee.

From Nova Scotia.

6. He was so poorly, he couldn't pull a sick whore off a piss pot.

126. WEALTH

1. He has more money than Irving has oil.
• This refers to New Brunswick's wealthy Irving family.

Shelley Timmons, North East Margaree, Inverness County, Nova Scotia

2. They're farting through silk now.
• They have newly acquired wealth.

Reino Kokkila, Etobicoke, Ontario

3. A shroud has no pockets.
• So you can't take your money with you. Therefore spend it now and be happy.

Sandra Morrison, Bury, Québec

127. WEATHER

Cold Weather & Winter

1. So cold this morning, before I could take a piss, I had to kick a hole in the air.

2. So cold you had to back up to pee. Or: So cold you had to pee walking backwards.
• Both these laments were heard in Saskatchewan.

3. It gets so cold in the Yukon, the salmon grow fur, and locals make slippers from them.

Shirley Dobie, Dawson Creek, British Columbia

4. It was so cold, the dogs chewed the putty off the windows.
• This is a translation from a regional French expression of the Saguenay Lac-St-Jean area of Québec, which in standard French might appear as *"Il faisait tellement froid que les chiens mâchaient le mastic après les fenêtres."*

James Selfe, Nun's Island, Québec

5. How cold is it? I just saw a red squirrel towing a whiskey-jack to get him started.
• A northern Ontario saying.

Edith Wheatley, Dryden, Ontario

6. It was so cold on the prairie last night that a farmer had his hands in his own pocket.

7. It's a tree-snappin' night.
• It's so cold up north that frost will get into the tree and split it. In some cases, the tree snaps or explodes producing a long, lightning-like rip in the bark. Snappin' cold refers to the way trees snap in below-zero temperatures.

Contributors: William Norman, London, Ontario, and Marjorie Andrews.

8. Not a fit day for a fence post.
• A very cold and stormy day in P.E.I.

9. We're takin' the mailbox in.
• There's going to be a violent ocean storm.

From Port Medway, Nova Scotia.

10. Colder than a well-digger's knee.

11. It's colder than a witch's tit in a cast-iron bra.

12. Cold as the icicle on a polar bear's dick.

13. It's cold as poor Willy, and he's pretty chilly; he's dead, poor bugger.

14. Cold as the snow on an Eskimo's bum.
• Offensive northern expression.

15. It's a two-squaw night.
• Offensive description of a cold evening.

Darkness

1. Darker than the inside of a black cow at midnight.

Dry Weather

1. So dry last week around Virden, frogs were poundin' on the screen door, askin' for a dipper of water.
• Virden is in southern Manitoba on the Saskatchewan border.

2. It's drier than a popcorn fart.
• Said of a hot summer in Alberta, but widespread across Canada to indicate dryness.
Also said by thirsty people: I'm drier than a popcorn fart.

3. It's so dry in southern Alberta, the trees go lookin' for the dogs.

4. It's so dry, mice have to pack a lunch to cross a field.

Keith and Christie Funk-Froese, Rosenfeld, Manitoba

5. It's so dry a cow's gotta graze ten miles an hour just to keep ahead of the dust.
• Saskatchewan saying.

6. Well's so low we'll have to start haulin' water to it.

Fair Weather

1. There's enough blue sky to make a Dutchman a pair of britches.

Jean Gibson, Thunder Bay, Ontario

2. We've a month on the days.
• Nova S. Bannerman, named after an aunt, Nova Scotia Sim, believes this Canadian saying is unique to Barney's River Station in Pictou County. Nova writes that "after the first hard month of winter is safely over one hears this being said, with a considerable degree of satisfaction."

3. Some day on a line of clothes.
• This Newfoundland expression suggests a warm, sunny, blowy day, perfect for drying.

From Jacqueline Hanrahan.

4. Let's stamp the robin.
• On seeing the first robin of spring, one licks one's right wrist with the tongue and pats the lick with the left hand, to bring good luck and fine weather.
• William Norman of London, Ontario, reports this innocent superstition from southern Ontario.

5. They're out today in their figures.
• That is, folks have taken off their bulky winter clothes and now in fair weather one can see what their bodies look like.

Hot Weather

1. Hot as a June bride in a feather bed.

2. It's hotter than the hubs of Hades.

3. It's hotter than the bottom of Gandhi's sandal.
• A Maritime weather comment sent in by Xenia Zafiris.

4. So hot I'm sweatin' like a two-dollar toilet.
  Lloyd Grahame, Kingsville, Ontario

5. So hot the hens are layin' hard-boiled eggs.

6. Hot enough to fry spit.

7. Hotter than a whore's doorknob on payday.

Rain

1. It's damper than duck dung.
• Said of Vancouver weather.

2. Q: Do you think it's going to rain?
   A: Be a helluva dry summer if it don't.

3. Of heavy rain: Like a two-assed cow pissing on a flat rock.
  Katherine Koller, Edmonton, Alberta

4. During a heavy rain in a 1940s Vancouver Island logging camp: Hope the old lady remembered to let the dog in.

5. Of an all-day light rain: It's a Scotch mist to wet an Irishman to the hide.
• John Boyd of Silver City, New Mexico, remembers his Scottish mother saying this at Oak Mountain and Peel, New Brunswick.

6. It's comin' up a bad cloud.

7. Enough rain to choke a toad.

8. It's so wet we're shooting ducks in the pantry.

Snow

1. The old woman is pluckin' her geese today.
• Said of a fluffy snowfall. R.M. Lawson was told this one by a great-grandmother who owned a general store in Burford, Ontario. She had heard it first in 1889. But, interestingly, this is a direct translation of a Ukrainian folk-saying that also shows up in Manitoba earlier in the 19th century.

2. Of a blizzard in southern Alberta: It's a real snit storm. Half *sn*ow and half sh*it*.

3. Of a fluffy snowfall: She's driftin' down like dinner plates.

   D.W. Bone, Wartime, Saskatchewan

4. When it snows while the sun is shining: The devil's wife is fluffing her pillows.

   From White Head, Guysborough County, Nova Scotia.

Storms

1. It's storming so bad, the birds are walking.

2. It's a poor day to set a hen.

3. Least there's no flies out today.
• Items 2 and 3 are said humorously during a violent storm in P.E.I.

Various Weather Conditions

1. Of Canadian weather in general: Nine months of winter and three months of darn hard sleddin'.

   Gordon Dysart, Espanola, Ontario

2. Water's flatter than a plate of puppy pee.
   • British Columbia boaters' slang. Newfoundland slang has the zippier variant "flatter than a plate of piss."

3. *Le diâble est aux vaches.* 'The devil's in the cows.'
   • In Québec, it means the weather will change soon.

4. There's a circus around the moon.
   • Said of a lunar halo.

5. *Le temps a viré comme une anse de cruche* 'the weather's turned like the handle on a jug.'

6. Such a pea-souper, sailors could sit on the ship's rail and lean against the fog.
   • Royal Canadian Navy expression from the Second World War.

   John G. Jarvis, Calgary, Alberta

Wind

1. Blowin' a gagger.
   • Ontario expression to describe a north wind blowing south off Georgian Bay.

2. That wind is strong enough to blow the nuts off a gang plough.
   • Said of a Saskatchewan storm. Many variants exist, for example, from New Brunswick: Wind strong enough to blow the nuts off the Miramichi bridge.

They are all probably based on: Cold enough to freeze the nuts off a brass monkey. Incidentally, there is not, in all the annals of British naval lexicography, one single printed record or reference of any piece of naval ordnance named a "brass monkey." It was never an object that held cannonballs on a war ship. The expression means just what it says: if a monkey was made of brass, this cold would crack the brass. All the reputed etymologies that claim an origin in the British navy for this expression are to be viewed with suspicion.

3. The wind is blowin' and it's too lazy to go around you.

4. It was so windy, my hen laid the same egg twice.

5. It's a cold wind to calf your ass up against.

6. You can always tell people from Saskatchewan. When the wind stops blowing, they fall over.

7. It's windy enough to blow the horns off a bull.
• Direct translation of Canadian French: *Il vente assez fort pour écorner un boeuf.*

   Guy Charbonneau, Timmins, Ontario

128. WELCOME

1. Welcome as a turd in a punch bowl.

2. *Reçu comme un chien dans un jeu de quilles.*
'Welcome as a dog in a bowling alley.'

129. WORK

1. Busy as a Halifax Harbour harlot, with the HMCS Toronto in port.

Wilhelmine Estabrook

2. I could jump down any shaft you ever dug, and not even break my ankle.
• From gold-mining slang of Timmins, Ontario.

3. He works harder than a dog under a covered wagon.
• During the settling of the prairies, homesteading drylanders drove covered wagons along trails. The wiser dogs raced alongside the wagon in the shadow cast by the brown tarp covering the wagon. It was cooler there than in full sun, and the dog could run along farther without tiring. Or — another correspondent suggests — the saying refers to the fact that dogs copulated under wagons.

4. *Avoir le trou de cul en dessus du bras.* 'To have your ass under your arm.'
• That is, to be dead-tired, in Québec.

5. This is not his first rodeo.
• He is competent at this job; he knows what he's doing.

Vivian Hansen, Calgary, Alberta

6. Come a horny onto her!
• From Nova Scotia's South Shore, this saying means 'to give something your best effort.'

Catherine Hiltz, Bridgewater, Nova Scotia

7. I can't piss and fart, and draw the cart, all at once!
• This reply is given when a person already busy is

asked to do something more. It was heard in the Star City area of Saskatchewan among homesteaders who had come north from Nebraska.

Contributed by Margarita Hill, of Prince Albert, Saskatchewan.

8. You'll soon see the rabbit.
• This Prince Edward Island folk saying implies that work is almost completed. When you cut hay beginning at the perimeter of a field, a rabbit in that field will run toward the centre. When there is no cover left, the rabbit bolts. This is T.K. Pratt's explanation in his splendid *Dictionary of Prince Edward Island English.*

9. Who will lift the cat's tail, if the cat won't?
• This is a direct translation from Finnish, and is still heard among descendants of immigrants from Finland in northern Ontario.

10. He doesn't ride the day he saddles.
• A translation from Danish, this is said of one who procrastinates. Collected near Delta, British Columbia.

11. A fish in the punt is worth two in the water.
• The punt is a boat. The basic Newfoundland meaning is: keep fishing, and don't complain about how small the catch is; recognize instead what you've caught so far.

12. Of strict foremen at lumber camps: So strict, you darsn't spit on the whippletree in them days.
• James Fairfield was in Minden, Ontario, in the 1940s and remembered conditions in local lumber camps at the turn of the century. Submitted by his

nephew, George Fairfield of Toronto. A whippletree or whiffletree is the bar, of wood or steel, that swings on a pivot and to which the traces of a harness are fastened, so that a vehicle or farm implement can be pulled by horses or oxen. Because of its position between the animal and the driver, it produces one of the oldest farm jokes in North America:

Question by cityslicker: What's a whiffletree?

Answer by farmer: Now any horse's ass would know that!

13. The best fertilizer for the soil is the farmer's footprints.

14. You can't live on the wind and roost on the clothesline all of the time.
• This was said in rebuke to children who complained of doing chores on the farm.

Martha Jackson, Toronto

15. He's always puttin' things off. Why, he didn't get a birthmark until he was seven.

16. Tired? If my arsehole drags any lower, I'll have to stick it in the cuff of my pants.

17. I'm sweating like a hen drawing rails.
• Chopping down cedar trees and then drawing them with a team of horses out of the bush, perhaps to make fence posts and rails, is sweaty work for a human being, and would be quite strenuous for a chicken! Domestic fowl are subject to heat stroke too. Variant: Hotter than a hen drawing rails in July.

18. Harder than pushing your truck uphill with a rope.

Don Shanahan, Brighton, Ontario

19. A new broom sweeps clean, but it takes an old one to get in the corners.

20. I was picking shit in the henhouse with a wooden beak.
• Said of any messy chore.

Teresa and Jerry Sinkowski, Waterford, Ontario

E.C. Lougheed of Guelph sent this variant to describe tedious labour:

Might as well get a tin beak and pick corn with the hens.

21. As busy as a hound covering turds in long grass.

22. As busy as a one-armed paperhanger with hives.

23. A man who watches the clock remains one of the hands.

24. *Occupé comme une queue de veau dans le temps des mouches.* 'To be busy as a calf's tail in fly time.'

25. That's as easy as stuffing soft shit up a wildcat's ass with the narrow end of a toothpick.

26. Busier than a bee in a vacuum cleaner.
• This is a modern version of a very old saying. Thomas Jefferson left Washington at the end of his second Presidential term in 1809 and never returned to the capitol. When asked about his seventeen years of retirement, he said he had been "as busy as a bee in a molasses barrel."

27. Even if it's only the breath of your arse, do it well.
• Advice to a young man starting his first job.

28. Never say "whoa" in a bad spot.

29. She's busier than a two-headed cat in a creamery.

From Three Hills, Alberta.

30. Careful! Don't strain your milk.
• One woman to another doing strenuous work.
  Pamela Miller, Apsley, Ontario

31. I'm as busy as a blue-assed fly.

32. Tiredness: As pooped as a lumber-camp whore the morning after payday.

33. You get paid the same for marching as you do for fighting.
• This is soldiers' slang from the Second World War.
  Gerry Sauvé, Gibsons, British Columbia

34. Busier than a cat burying shit on a marble floor.
  Monica Allison, Winnipeg, Manitoba

35. Busy as a whore working two beds.

36. Make yourself useful instead of ornamental.
  Ruth MacDonald, St. Catharines, Ontario

37. I've been busy as a bee in a molasses barrel.
• This one is so old that Thomas Jefferson said it. He often used it to answer visitors to Monticello, who wondered what he had been doing during the seventeen years he had been absent from national politics. For Jefferson had left Washington at the end of his second presidential term and retired to his Virginia farm, never to return to political life.

38. Just because you got a crack in your ass, don't make you a cripple.
• When asked to fetch something for someone else, with the implied command: Get it yourself!
  Keith Bird, Viscount, Saskatchewan

39. Don't bust a gusset.
• Don't work too hard, and split the seams of your clothing, particularly a gusset, a piece of triangular cloth inserted in a seam to expand or reinforce it.

Kate O'Donnell, Rainbow Lake, Alberta

40. Fetch in the wood and water while you're resting.
• Angus McAuley of Surrey, British Columbia, recalls his grandmother's bit of Gaelic canniness when urging her grandsons to bring in water from a well and wood for the stove at noon, just before washing up for lunch.

41. Gone to fetch a basket of water.
• That is, sent on a useless errand.

130. THE END

1. Marjorie Andrews recalls a neighbour named Old Jack who always said, when the final whistle had ended a Saturday Night hockey game on radio or TV, "It's all over, Mary; pull down your dress."

2. Audrey Godbout of Cap Rouge, Québec, recalls this bit of revisionist Christianity. "May the love of the Lord follow you all the days of your life," said Great Grandma, as the gossipy neighbour finally left the house. Grandma would close the door, adding, "and never catch up with you."

3. It's just like wiping your ass with a hoop. There's no end to it.

A Final Word to the Reader

Had a laugh about *anything* Canadian lately? I hope you did chuckle and snort during the perusal of these sayings. I did while compiling this trove, succumbing to wet guffaws, giggles best suppressed in a locker room, and even thigh-slappers that might raise welts on a corpse!

Readers supplied many of the most cracklingly funny sayings for this book. A reader in Sault Ste. Marie, Ontario, heard this one in the 1940s: "You smell better than a dime whore on nickel Tuesday." A localism from Prince Edward Island describes a very small crowd: "There were thousands and thousands from Tyne Valley alone." From Three Hills, Alberta, comes: "He's lower than a snake's belly in a wagon rut."

Not all our folk expressions hark back to a rural past, although some of the best do. An ecologist from British Columbia said of a dull companion: "He's got his solar panels on the north side." When an audiophile breaks wind, he might hear: "Not bad for a half-inch woofer." "They eat like gannets" say people on Cape Sable Island, Nova Scotia, to describe those who bolt their food whole, as gannets swallow fish whole. An Albertan outdoors guide, asked how things are going, replies, "Slicker than a brookie!" Brookie is a Canadian diminutive for brook trout. And Canadians are adept at sexual sayings. "Noisier than inbreeding on a cornhusk mattress." "With him, every night was like hormone day at a mink ranch." "He has a one-track mind, and that's narrow gauge" runs an old Canadian railroader's insult. In Saskatchewan, a storm prompted: "That wind is strong enough to blow the nuts off a gang plough." A north wind streaming south off Georgian Bay summons the comment: "It's blowin' a gagger." Too pooped to participate is translated into this Prairie lament: "If my arsehole drags any lower, I'll have to stick it in the cuff of my pants."

If you know truly Canadian sayings both vivid and memorable, and you did not find them listed in this book, send them along to the address below. Do give the circumstance and location in Canada when you first heard the saying. And perhaps your name will appear in the next edition of *Canadian Sayings?*

Bill Casselman
205 Helena Street,
Dunnville, Ontario, Canada
N1A 2S6

MORE BILL CASSELMAN BOOKS ABOUT CANADIAN WORDS
FROM McARTHUR & COMPANY

CASSELMAN'S CANADIAN WORDS

In this #1 Best-Seller, Bill Casselman delights and startles with word stories
from every province and territory of Canada. Did you know that . . .?
Scarborough means "Harelip's Fort." The names of **Lake Huron &
Huronia** stem from a vicious, racist insult. Huron in old French meant 'long-
haired clod.' French soldiers labeled the Wendat people with this nasty mis-
nomer in the 1600s. **To deke out** is a Canadian verb that began as hockey
slang, short for 'to decoy an opponent.' Canada has a fish that ignites. On our
Pacific coast, the oolichan or **candle fish** is so full of oil it can be lighted at
one end and used as a candle. "**Mush! Mush!** On, you huskies!" cried Sergeant
Preston of The Yukon to 1940s radio listeners, thus introducing a whole gen-
eration of Canucks to the word once widely used in the Arctic to spur on sled
dogs. Although it might sound like a word from Inuktitut, early French trap-
pers first used it, borrowing the term from the Canadian French command to
a horse to go: *marche! marche!* Yes, it's Québécois for giddyap!

All these and more fascinating terms from Canadian place names, politics,
sports, plants and animals, clothing. Everything from Canadian monsters to
mottoes is here.

Casselman's Canadian Words
ISBN 1-55278-032-5
224 pages, illustrated, $19.95

CASSELMANIA: MORE WACKY CANADIAN WORDS & SAYINGS

Should you purchase a copy of Casselmania? Below, dear reader, is a quiz to try. If you pass, buy Casselmania. If you fail, buy two copies!

1. "Slackers" is a nickname for what Canadian city?
(a) Vancouver
(b) Halifax
(c) Sackville, New Brunswick
Answer: (b) Halifax. Why "Slackers?" Because often when Canadian Navy crews put in to Halifax harbour, the sailors had some "slack" time for shore-leave.

2. Eh? is a true marker of Canadian speech. But which of the following authors uses eh? exactly as Canadians now use it.
(a) Emily Brontë in *Wuthering Heights*.
(b) Charles Dickens in *Bleak House*.
(c) Geoffrey Chaucer in *The Canterbury Tales* in 1400 A.D.

Answer: All of the above! "Eh?" is almost 1,000 years old as an interjection in Old English, Middle English, and, of course, in modern Canadian English too.

3. The first Skid Row or Skid Road in Canada was in Vancouver at the end of the 19th century. The term originated because
(a) alcoholics kept slipping in the muddy streets
(b) out-of-work loggers drank in cheap saloons at the end of a road used to skid logs
(c) cheap houses were moved on skids to slummy areas
Answer: (b). Skids were greased logs used to slide rough timber to a water-way or railhead. There was a skid road in Vancouver, where unemployed log-gers waited for jobs, and took the odd bottle of liquid refreshment.

4. In central Ontario, a gorby is
(a) one who follows Russian politics
(b) one who thinks Mike Harris is good for the province
(c) a tourist
Answer (c). A localism in the central Ontario tourist area of Muskoka is "gorby" used by some inhabitants of the area, mostly younger people, to describe loud tourists of the yahoo persuasion. "Oh-oh. Another busload of gorbies!" The origin of gorby is, I believe, in the 1950s camping slang term G.O.R.P., an acronym for Good Old Raisins and Peanuts, a trail mix suitable for canoe nibbling, easily packed, and not subject to immediate spoilage.

Casselmania: More Wacky Canadian Words & Sayings
ISBN 1-55278-035-X
298 pages, illustrated, $19.95

CANADIAN GARDEN WORDS

Trowel in hand, Bill Casselman digs into the loamy lore and fascinating facts about how we have named the plants that share our Dominion. But are there *Canadian* Garden Words? Yes! Try those listed below.

Camas Lily. A bulb grown all over the world for its spiky blue flowers. The name arose in British Columbia where First Peoples cooked and ate the bulbs. Camas means 'sweet' in Nootka, a Pacific Coast language. The original name of Victoria on Vancouver Island was Camosun, in Nootka 'place where we gather camas bulbs.'

A Snotty Var is a certain species of fir tree in Newfoundland. Why? Find out in *Canadian Garden Words*.

Mistletoe! So Christmassy. The word means 'poop on a stick.' Oops! Look within for a bounty of surprising origins of plant names. Orchid means 'testicle' in Greek. So does avocado. While plant names have come into English from dozens of world languages, Bill Casselman has found the Canadian connection to 100s of plant names and garden lore and packed his new, September '97 book with them.

Casselman reports on Canadian plant names and on the origin of all the common trees and flowers that decorate our gardens from Fogo Island to Tofino, B.C.

Canadian Garden Words
ISBN 1-55278-036-8
356 pages, illustrated, $19.95